Matthew Henson,
Black Explorer

Other Books by the Author

Matthew Henson

Matthew Henson, Black Explorer

Edward F. Dolan, Jr.

Illustrated with photographs

DODD, MEAD & COMPANY
New York

Illustration Credits

Reproduced from the collection of the Library of Congress, 121, 122, 126, 132, 135, 137, 143, 151, 155, 157, 162, 165; United Press International Photo, 177, 178; from *Northward Over the Great Ice* by Robert E. Peary, Vols. I and II, 1898, 20, 23, 24, 29, 30, 34, 37, 47, 48, 50, 55, 61, 66, 68, 71, 72. The frontispiece is from the collection of the Explorers Club. Maps on pages 73, 96, 124, and 146 are by the author.

Copyright © 1979 by Edward F. Dolan, Jr.
All rights reserved
No part of this book may be reproduced in any form
without permission in writing from the publisher
Printed in the United States of America

1   2   3   4   5   6   7   8   9   10

Library of Congress Cataloging in Publication Data

Dolan, Edward F   date
  Matthew Henson, Black explorer.

  Bibliography: p.
  Includes index.
  SUMMARY: A biography of the black explorer who accompanied Robert E. Peary to the North Pole in 1909.
  1. Henson, Matthew Alexander, 1866–1955—Juvenile literature.   2. North Pole—Juvenile literature.
3. Explorers—United States—Biography—Juvenile literature.   [1. Henson, Matthew Alexander, 1866–1955.   2. Explorers.   3. Afro-Americans—Biography]   I. Title.
G635.H4D64   919.8 [B]   [92]   79–52053
ISBN 0–396–07728–5

*This book is for
my brother, Michael*

Contents

Matthew Henson, Black Explorer

1.

Looking for Adventure

MATT HENSON braked the sledge to a halt. After all the miles of steady walking in the cold air, he leaned against the upstanders and breathed deeply. Up ahead, his dog team settled gratefully down on the ice to rest. Today's march across the frozen Arctic Ocean had been a good one.

Strung out in a line were six sledges, manned by two white men, a black, and a half-dozen Eskimos. Long a good judge of distances, Matt felt certain that they had come to within 150 miles of the North Pole, the very roof of the world. This was March 30, 1909, and they had been battling their way over the rough ice for a solid month now.

Matt straightened, his breathing steady again. He was a slender man of medium height, forty-two years old. Beneath his fur jacket, his muscles were hard but supple; long years of Arctic exploration with Robert E. Peary had made them that way. He had a broad face, with a prominent nose and wide-set eyes. His skin was the color of well-rubbed copper. He was the black man in the group.

Though his breathing was steady, Matt was anything but calm. He knew that today's march had brought him to one of the most critical moments in his life. All his work with Peary might come to an end in the next few moments. Or he might get the signal to push on with the explorer toward the honor that Peary had been seeking for years—the honor of being the first man in history to reach the North Pole.

Matt saw Peary walking past from his own sledge at the rear of the line. Peary smiled a greeting, but kept on moving, heading for the lead sledge. There, pickaxe in hand, stood wiry and stubby Bob Bartlett. For days now, Bartlett had been in the lead position, hacking a path through the jumbled ice for the expedition to follow. Peary, well over six feet tall, towered above Bartlett as the two of them began to talk.

Well, Matt thought, we're the last two of his own men, Bob. The choice is down to between the two of us.

There might be just a handful of men on the Arctic Ocean ice at present. But there had been five whites, one black, and seventeen Eskimos with Peary when he began his march northward a month ago. He had never planned, however, to have all the men go clear to the Pole with him. Their sledges, loaded with food supplies, were meant only to get him as close to his destination as possible, at which point he would make a final push with a few select companions. They would be the men who had the most strength left after all the miles of travel.

And so, as the supplies were consumed over the days, the empty sledges had been returned to the base camp down on Ellesmere Island. With them had gone the most exhausted of the men, Americans and Eskimos alike. Each time Peary singled out the ones to be sent back, Matt had held his breath. He'd been exhausted, his endurance stretched right to the limit, and he was sure that Peary would soon look in his direction.

But he'd survived the weeding-out process and had continued to sledge northward, hardly believing his good fortune. He wanted desperately to be chosen for the final party. It would be such a fitting climax to all the years of work with Peary—work that had taken them first to the jungles of Nicaragua, then to Greenland's windswept icecap, and finally here to within reach of the North Pole.

It was work that had made Peary's name world-famous. And it was work that had transformed Matt from the man's personal servant to his assistant and had made him into a full-fledged Arctic explorer in his own right.

There was another, even more compelling, reason for wanting to be with the final party. All his adult life, Peary had dreamed of being the first man at the North Pole. Matt had devoted his own life to helping him realize that ambition. Now, if he could just keep going, he could realize a deep but never-voiced dream of his own: he could become the first *black* man in history ever to stand at the Pole.

Waiting at his sledge, he knew the time to choose the final party had come and that Peary was making the decision now. There was no chance that both he and Bartlett would travel the rest of the way with the explorer. One or the other would be needed to supervise the Eskimos who were to be sent back.

Matt felt his heart sinking as he watched Peary and Bartlett. Both were talking earnestly and Bartlett was nodding. Bartlett was an excellent traveler, tough and hard-working. And he seemed tireless. Surely, the choice was going to him.

Suddenly, Peary nodded, stepped away, and headed for Matt's sledge. Here it comes, Matt thought. The disappointment.

Matt steeled himself for the bad news. Then, before Peary got to him, he was remembering that he had always wanted adventure. He told himself that, even if he was to miss out on this greatest march of all, he'd still had more than his share of excitement in life. More than any other black man he knew and more than most white men.

One adventure after another, dating right back to his earliest childhood . . .

2.

The first of those adventures took place just a few months after he was born Matthew Alexander Henson on August 8, 1866. The Civil War had ended little more than a year earlier and his home state of Maryland was rocked with strife in its aftermath. Matt was too young to know what was happening, but the upheaval was frightening to his parents.

The Lemuel Hensons were tenant farmers who worked a small piece of land near the Potomac River, some forty-four miles south of Washington, D.C. The war hadn't freed them from slavery, for they had never been slaves to begin with; like so many of the black people in Maryland, they had been free-born. Nor did the war free those who *had* been in slavery. Maryland remained in the Union throughout the fighting and, consequently, was not affected by the Emancipation Proclamation, which applied only to the Confederate states.

A year later, however, Maryland abolished slavery on its own—and that was the action that triggered the strife. Slave owners there were furious over the loss of a cheap and valuable work force. They banded together to have the new law repealed. When they failed, their opposition to a state full of free blacks turned violent. Soon after the war ended, the Ku Klux Klan began riding, its aim being to suppress the blacks and see that they won neither social nor political power.

Black homes and farms were terrorized; some people were threatened, some beaten, and some killed; wooden crosses were set afire in barnyards; the skull and crossbones was painted on doors and walls. A worried Lemuel Henson and his wife watched what was going on. The Klan hadn't visited them yet, but they felt that their time was sure to come.

And so they left their farm and, carrying baby Matt in their arms, moved to Washington, D.C.

There, with the first adventure behind him, Matt lived until he was in his early teens. For some years, the family occupied a home in the Georgetown area, which at the time was a slum neighborhood. But, when his mother died and his father was unable to support him, Matt was placed with an uncle. The uncle welcomed the seven-year-old and enrolled him in the N Street School. Matt attended the school through the sixth grade.

The boy came in for a shock when he was thirteen. He learned that now his uncle could no longer afford to care for him. It would be necessary for him to leave school and the home he had known for so long. He couldn't go back to his father because Lemuel had died recently. For the first time in his life, as he would be for the rest of his days, Matt Henson was on his own.

To support himself, he got a job in a small restaurant owned by a black woman named Janey Moore. For a dollar a week, he started as a dishwasher, but, within a short time, was waiting on tables and helping with the cooking. Janey was a kind-hearted woman who, on finding that Matt had no home, set up a small cot for him in a warm corner of the kitchen. Matt worked at the restaurant for about nine months.

Throughout all that time, while stretched out on his cot at night, the boy wondered what he could do with his life. He had no ready answers. But he knew one thing for certain. No matter how kind Janey was, he didn't want to spend his life in the menial work that he was doing for her. Nor did he want to go on living in the poverty that he saw all around him in Georgetown. He wanted . . .

Matt struggled for the right words. Then he found them. He wanted to do something exciting. He wanted a life of adventure.

He stared up at the ceiling. But where to find it?

The answer came from one of the restaurant's frequent customers. Baltimore Jack cut a very dashing figure in his seaman's jacket and cap.

Born a slave, he'd early run off and had spent his life sailing the world. Aboard a string of merchant vessels, he'd been everywhere—China, Japan, Europe, India—and he was full of stories of all the ports he'd visited and the wonderful sights he'd seen. Matt listened, wide-eyed, and suddenly knew what he must do. He, too, must go to sea.

Once the decision was made, the boy acted immediately. He packed his few belongings in a sack and hugged the tearful Janey good-bye. Then down the road from Washington to the city of Baltimore and its great seaport he went.

On his arrival, he made his way to the docks. There, he found himself surrounded by all sorts of bustling activity, with a forest of masts swaying gently overhead. And there, he was struck with a terrible realization. He had absolutely no idea of how to go about finding a job as a sailor.

Matt later remembered himself as one very lucky fourteen-year-old that day. As things turned out, he didn't have to go looking for a job. The job came to him.

It happened when he stopped to gaze up at a trim three-master bearing the name *Katie Hines*; he thought she was the most beautiful sight he'd ever seen. A giant of a blue-eyed man was just coming down the ship's gangway to the dock and, on an impulse, Matt decided to ask him how work was to be found. The man listened, first with sympathy and then with admiration, while Matt explained that he had no family and had hiked all the way here from Washington.

By the time the story was finished, the listener found himself wanting to help this ragged black boy; courage of his sort deserved to be rewarded. The man introduced himself as Captain Childs, the master of the *Katie Hines*. He was sailing that very day, bound on a year-long voyage to China with a cargo of wheat. It just so happened that he was in need of a cabin boy . . .

That did it. Long before the *Katie Hines* raised sail with the tide, Matt had signed on as a crew member and was setting the Captain's table for dinner. It was his first job aboard a vessel that was to be his home—and his school—for the next five years.

They were a glorious five years. After the first China voyage, Matt graduated from cabin boy to able-bodied seaman. He grew into a hard-muscled young man as he sailed to ports in Japan, the Philippines, Africa, France, and Russia. He learned to work aloft, to read the weather, and to hold a steady course at the helm. Under the watchful eye of the ship's carpenter, he became an expert with hammer, saw, and plane.

On top of all else, he received a good, if informal, education from Captain Childs. The seaman had an excellent library in his cabin. He insisted that Matt spend a good deal of time with the books on its shelves—books that ranged from texts on geography, history, and mathematics to the works of Shakespeare, Sir Walter Scott, and Charles Dickens.

The good years ended suddenly when the aging Captain fell ill and died at sea during a homeward voyage in 1885. Nineteen-year-old Matt was heartbroken. He couldn't bear to remain aboard the *Katie Hines* under some other skipper, and so he said good-bye to the ship as soon as she docked at Baltimore. Within a few days, he took a berth on a fishing schooner bound for Newfoundland waters.

Now everything seemed to go wrong with his life. First, conditions aboard the schooner were so filthy—and the captain so cruel—that Matt quit at the first Canadian port and made his way back to the United States. Next, he told himself that he'd had enough of the sea for a while. He decided to put his carpentry skills to use and went looking for a job—only to run into his first real taste of racial prejudice.

He'd been too young to know the Ku Klux Klan and, in all his years aboard the *Katie Hines*, he'd been well treated. Most of the crewmen had liked the gritty youngster, with the few exceptions keeping their mouths shut because they knew Captain Childs looked on him as an adopted son. But now, as he went looking for work in one city after another, he found himself the victim of his color. No one could—or would—employ him. Carpenters were hired through a union, and the union did not permit blacks in its ranks.

Discouraged, Matt had to take on any kind of work that came his way.

He was a stevedore in Boston for a time. A night watchman in Buffalo. A messenger boy somewhere else. Then a common laborer. At last, wandering home to Washington, D.C., he landed a job as a stock clerk in the clothing and hat store of B. H. Steinmetz and Sons.

It was the best job he'd found in months. But he knew that it was far beneath his capabilities. The year was 1887 and he was twenty-one years old. Angrily, he wondered if this was to be his fate as a black man—a lifetime of stock clerking or of moving from one poor-paying job to another. Perhaps he should get back to sea again. If only he could find another *Katie Hines* . . .

Then it happened. Without warning. As on that morning when he'd stopped to gaze up at a beautiful ship, his life changed. Robert Edwin Peary came into the Steinmetz store.

3.

Mr. Steinmetz was obviously expecting the young Navy officer who entered that November day. Immediately, without waiting to hear what the customer needed, he summoned Matt and told him to fetch a selection of tropical helmets. Lieutenant Peary, he added excitedly, was soon to escape Washington's cold weather.

Matt disappeared into the stock room for a few minutes. As he was returning, he could hear Steinmetz talking and the words, heard just faintly, puzzled him. He couldn't be certain, but he thought the man was saying, "Matt's the young fellow I was telling you about. You wouldn't be making a mistake . . ." Then, when Matt deposited a stack of helmets on the counter and started back to his other duties, Peary gave him a close, penetrating look and asked him to stay.

It was all very puzzling. And it grew even more puzzling when, after trying on several helmets and finally selecting one, Peary turned again to him. Matt found himself being closely studied by this tall, slender man with the sharp blue-gray eyes. Peary seemed to be making up his mind about something. He had a lean face, a sweeping mustache, and reddish hair that washed across his forehead to curl—almost theatrically—above his right temple. Matt guessed him to be in his early thirties.

Then, as if coming to a decision, Peary began to speak and the mystery was soon solved. Explaining that he was with the Navy's Civil Engineer Corps, he said that he'd just been assigned to lead an engineering survey team to Nicaragua. As part of his pay, he was to be given a personal servant to take along.

It so happened that he had met his friend, Mr. Steinmetz, on the street the other day. They'd talked about the clothing he needed to buy for the trip and then he had mentioned that he was looking for someone to fill the servant's job. Mr. Steinmetz had immediately recommended Matt . . .

As Matt was listening, his mind was clicking over. At the mention of Nicaragua, he understood the reason for the survey. The United States, he knew from the newspapers, was one of several countries interested in laying a canal across Central America to connect the Atlantic and Pacific oceans. Just now, the French were already working on a canal, trying to dig it across the Isthmus of Panama and running into all sorts of trouble. The United States thought that a better route could be found to the north, through Nicaragua. Obviously, Lieutenant Peary was being sent to look for it.

Peary's next words came through Matt's thoughts. The survey will take six months to complete. The life won't be easy because the work is to be done in a region of swamps and jungles. The servant's pay will be $20 a month, plus board. If Matt takes the job, he'll be able to come back to the Steinmetz store on his return.

Now that he'd had a look at him, Peary said that he felt Matt would be a good choice. But is Matt interested? If so, he'll have to be ready to leave in two weeks.

Indeed he was interested! Actually, he didn't care for the idea of being a servant. But that was unimportant. What counted was that, once again, adventure had come barging into his life. And, as usual, with no advance warning.

And so, in late November, 1887, Matt sailed down the Atlantic with

Peary and thirty-five engineers. The ship swung into the Caribbean and moved on to the Gulf of Mexico, pausing along the way at Jamaica to recruit 100 black laborers. The voyage ended on December 9 when the ship came up to the eastern coast of Nicaragua. Peary and his men went ashore at the small city of San Juan del Norte (later to have its name changed to Greytown).

En route, Matt learned that this was Peary's second trip to Nicaragua. In 1884, the young officer had served as second-in-command on a survey that had marked out a general route for the canal. Now, promoted to the position of chief engineer, he was back to check out a welter of details about the route.

Matt could understand why Peary had been placed in charge. His employer struck him as the most dedicated, thorough, and tireless worker he'd ever seen. After setting up base camp on an island beyond town, the Lieutenant immediately divided his engineers into surveying crews and sent them into the field with orders to lay out a path for a railroad along the canal route; the tracks would be needed to transport men and materials when construction of the canal began. Then he himself plunged into the swamps and jungles with the Jamaican laborers. Basically, he was out to do two things—probe the ground for spots firm enough to support the canal locks, and check the watershed to make absolutely sure that there was water enough for a canal.

As for Matt, he was instructed to remain at base camp and keep Peary's living quarters in good order. He not only did so but also improved the accommodations by putting his carpentry skills to use and building a work table and several bookcases for the Lieutenant. Whenever Peary came in from the field, caked with mud from head to foot, Matt washed his clothes, cleaned his boots, and made sure that the man was fed some very square meals.

Matt had to admit that this wasn't the kind of adventure that he'd wanted in Nicaragua. He wished that he could be out in the field with Peary. But he shrugged philosophically. Life in camp might be pretty dull at times, but it was certainly more exciting than in the Steinmetz store. At least, there were the wilds on all sides to be explored in his off hours.

Matt, however, didn't remain at base camp for long. One day, Peary hurried in from an inspection tour of the survey crews. He said that a member of one crew had just stumbled into some quicksand. The man had been pulled to safety immediately, but the experience had so unnerved him that he'd quit on the spot. Peary had no one to replace him—except Matt.

From that time on, Matt worked in the jungles and swamps as a rear chainman with the crew. It was his job to hold one end of a long chain steadily in place while the chain was stretched out to give the surveyors a straight line along which to sight and measure distances. The job was new to him, but he paid close attention to the crew leader and learned his duties quickly. By the time the crew finished its work months later, the leader had nothing but praise for Matt.

Never once, the man said, had his chainman done anything but concentrate on his job. And not once had he ever complained about the heat, the mud, the insects.

Matt found out about this praise after the survey was completed in June, 1888, and he was sailing home. As he was standing at the ship's rail one day, he looked up to find Peary at his side. The Lieutenant told him what the crew leader had said and then thanked him for all his work.

It was with an effort that Matt kept a look of surprise out of his face. In all the past months, Peary had been a good employer but never an especially friendly one. He'd always been fair and polite in his dealings, but he'd maintained a distance between himself and Matt—the distance of employer to servant. At first, Matt had thought that the Lieutenant might not like his color. Then he'd changed his mind. Peary was the same way with everyone. He was simply, by nature, an aloof man.

In his heart, Matt knew that he'd done good work and had proved himself to be far more than a mere servant. And he knew that all the men had done a good job. In seven months, they'd surveyed and checked the entire width of Nicaragua and had relocated several major sections of the canal route. When the canal finally took shape, it would be built on good ground.

(As matters turned out, the work went for nothing. The Nicaragua canal never became a reality. Within a few years, the French abandoned their digging to the south and, in 1902, the Americans took over for them, with the interocean canal finally cutting its way across the Isthmus of Panama.)

Though Matt knew he had done well, it was still good to hear Peary say so. But Peary didn't stop there. He leaned on the rail, stared out at the sea, and said that he was planning to do a future work of his own. He was planning to explore a part of the world as far removed in character from steaming Nicaragua as it could be. He was planning to explore the Arctic.

And he would like Matt to come along with him, again as his servant —and as an assistant.

Now there was no hiding Matt's surprise. His eyebrows flew up. Once again, his life was taking a sudden and unexpected turn. Opening before him was a new adventure.

He didn't know it then, but it was an adventure that would last for more than twenty years and finally, on a day at the end of March, 1909, bring him to within 150 miles of the North Pole.

2. Greenland
1891-1892

The Plan

THERE was nothing new about Robert Peary's interest in the Arctic. It had started when, as a little boy, he would sit nestled against his mother's side while she read him stories. One story concerned the American doctor, Elisha Kent Kane. In the 1850s, Kane had explored the far northern reaches of Greenland's west coast. The great Kane Basin up there was named for him.

The story of Kane's adventures—of how his men had taken axes and chopped the ice away so that his ships could advance through the frozen sea—fascinated the young Peary. He asked to hear it again and again. Then, when he was a little older, he read Kane's book, *Arctic Explorations*, and followed it with the works of other Polar greats.

Peary's interest in the Arctic lingered at the back of his mind throughout his boyhood and youth. Born at Cresson, Pennsylvania, on May 6, 1856, he was taken to Maine at age three and grew up there. Known as a "lone wolf" to his family and friends, he early showed a love of the outdoors. He was an avid camper and hiker by ten. His nature collections were crammed with seashells, pressed flowers, and birds' eggs and nests. In his early teens, he took up taxidermy as a hobby. He became so skilled that he was soon mounting animals for hunters living as far away as New York City.

Hoping for a life of outdoor adventure as a surveyor, Peary went to study engineering at Maine's Bowdoin College when he was seventeen. But he was in for a disappointment upon his graduation four years later, in 1877. Surveying work was so scarce that he finally had to take a job as a draftsman with the Coast and Geodetic Survey in Washington, D.C. He hated the job because it kept him anchored to a drawing board the whole day long.

Adventure, however, started to come his way in 1881 when he joined the Navy as a civil engineer and was given the rank of Lieutenant. He was ordered, first, to Key West, Florida, where he helped with the construction of a large dock. Then, because his superiors were so impressed with his work, he was sent on that first surveying trip to Nicaragua.

There was plenty of adventure in Nicaragua. It should have been enough to make any young man happy. But not Robert Peary. It just didn't fully satisfy him.

Why? Because there was another part of his nature that was being frustrated. He was an ambitious man who, to put it simply, wanted to become world-famous. The Navy was giving him adventure, yes. He was winning a reputation as a courageous and hard-working officer. But he was coming nowhere near the kind of fame that he craved. For years now, he had wondered just what he could do to put his name in the history books for all time to come.

Quite by accident, he got his answer shortly after returning to Washington, D.C., from the first Nicaragua trip. One night, he dropped into a secondhand bookstore in search of something to read. There, while browsing among the shelves, he came across a pamphlet by the Swedish explorer, Baron Nils Nordenskiold. It was called *Exploration of Interior Greenland*.

Suddenly, the old and loved story of Elisha Kent Kane flashed into mind, along with all the other Polar adventures he had read as a boy. And, just as suddenly, he was thinking of the North Pole. The very top of the world—an invisible point in a sea of shifting, treacherous ice—it had been attracting venturesome men from many countries for centuries now.

At first, back in the 1500s, they had thought that trading ships might reach the fabulous ports of the Orient by sailing across the North Pole. Later, they had found that such voyages would be impossible. They had then come to see the Pole as a great geographical prize, one quite as great as the South Pole and the crown of Mount Everest, and they had wanted the honor of being the first to stand there. As yet, no one had been able to claim that honor.

Peary stared at the pamphlet with unseeing eyes. What a place in history he could win for himself if he could succeed where all others had failed.

Actually, it wasn't the first time he'd thought about conquering the Pole. But, in the past, it had been no more than a boyish daydream. Now, even as he stood there in the bookstore, he could feel it hardening into an all-consuming ambition. He knew that he'd found the work of his life.

In the next days, after the first flush of enthusiasm had faded, Peary took a realistic look at his new ambition. He had to admit that it seemed preposterous at times. What hope did an obscure Navy Lieutenant in his late twenties have of reaching the North Pole?

For one thing, Arctic expeditions cost a great deal of money, money that he himself didn't have. He'd have to raise it from the government, or from someone or some organization interested in exploration. But he had no Arctic experience—had never even been near the place. Who would invest thousands of dollars in an untested newcomer?

The question didn't deter Peary. He'd just have to get the necessary experience. As a start, he read all that he could find on Arctic history and made endless notes on it; out of his study came the first of many ideas on how best to run an expedition and how best to survive in the brutal cold. Then, to gain some practical experience, he decided to visit Greenland.

Lying across Baffin Bay to the north and east of Canada, this Danish possession was one of the world's most rugged, desolate, and fascinating lands. Its coast was mountainous, with fiords knifing into it everywhere. Rising land stretched inland for anywhere from five to twenty-five miles and then disappeared—disappeared beneath a giant icecap that covered the rest of the country. Built up through the ages by accumulating snows, the cap was a vast shield that spread out for thousands of square miles and rose to elevations of eight to ten thousand feet. Buried beneath it were entire mountains and their valleys. It was Peary's intention to test himself by climbing up onto the icecap.

In 1886, the budding explorer obtained a six-months' leave from the Navy, booked passage aboard a Canadian whaler, and sailed for Greenland, arriving at Disko Bay on the southwestern coast in early June. He spent the next weeks climbing to the icecap and then moving out as far as he could onto that blinding field of white. Accompanying him was Christian Maigaard, a young Danish official stationed at Disko Bay. By mid-July, just before a blizzard drove them back, they reached an altitude of 7,500 feet.

So far as they knew, no man before them had ever traveled to that height on the cap.

It was an excited Peary who returned to the Navy late in the year. He had loved every minute of the Greenland trip. Even the blizzard—and a raging thing it had been—hadn't daunted him. He wanted to get back to Greenland as soon as possible for further training, this time at the head of an expedition of several men.

But now he was faced with the problem of raising funds to outfit a regular expedition. He'd gained some valuable experience, yes, but he couldn't ask anyone to sponsor a trip meant to do nothing but give him some more training. He'd have to have a definite exploration in mind, one that would excite the imaginations of the people and organizations with the money he needed.

The Navy, however, didn't give him the chance to come up with any ideas. His superiors handed him a new assignment. He was to go to Nicaragua on a second Canal survey. Soon after receiving his orders, he walked into the Steinmetz store and into the life of a young black man who, just as much as he, yearned for adventure.

2.

By the time Peary was sailing home from Nicaragua in 1888, he had hit upon the perfect plan for a Greenland expedition. It was there, crystal clear in his mind, when he asked if Matt would like to go to the Arctic as his servant and assistant in the near future.

Stunned by the offer, Matt listened to the plan in broad outline. No one, Peary said, had ever traveled all the way across the Greenland icecap. He was out to become the first man in history to do so. He'd start on the western side and would end up, God willing, staring out at the Atlantic Ocean. The crossing would be made at a point somewhere below Disko Bay so that he could take advantage of the country's narrowness as it approached its southern tip.

Matt quickly said that he'd be pleased and honored to accompany Peary. Peary replied with the promise to send for Matt as soon as the plans for the expedition were set.

From stunned surprise to anticipation: that was the course run by Matt's feelings in the next months at the Steinmetz store. After the excitement of the Canal work, he had dreaded going back to the routine of stock clerking. But now life was bearable. There was a new adventure looming just over the horizon.

Matt's reading of the newspaper told him that both happiness and disappointment visited Peary soon after the return home. There was happiness when the young officer married Josephine Diebitsch on August 11. Josephine, so the wedding notice said, was the daughter of Professor Herman H. Diebitsch of the Smithsonian Institution in Washington, D.C. Peary had courted her since their first meeting at a party three years ago.

Then disappointment came in a newspaper story at the end of September. It reported that a young Norwegian by the name of Fridtjof Nansen had just done precisely what Peary had hoped to do: he'd crossed the Greenland icecap. Matt stared at the headline and the lines of type underneath. Without warning—and perhaps without even knowing of the American's existence—Nansen had shattered Peary's great plan. No one would want to finance the second man to cross the icecap.

For a time, Matt wondered if Peary would recover from the blow. Or would this disappointment put an end to his Arctic career before it really got started? Then Matt shook his head. No. It didn't have a chance of doing *that*. He knew his man. Peary would think of something else.

Matt's faith was justified months later when, in January, 1891, he received a letter from Peary, who was now stationed at the League Island Navy Yard in Philadelphia. Peary wrote that he had replaced the first Greenland plan with a better one and had spent the past months raising money for the expedition. Things were just about ready to go. He needed Matt's help during the final preparations.

Peary added that he couldn't afford to pay Matt a salary himself. But he'd gotten him placed on the Navy payroll as his personal messenger. Could Matt come to Philadelphia right away?

In answer, Matt boarded a train for Pennsylvania. Soon, he was in Peary's office and listening to the new plan. Peary admitted that Nansen's crossing had knocked him flat for a time. But he'd bounced back. All right, he'd told himself, so you won't be the first man to cross the cap. But there's another, even better crossing that can be made . . .

Nansen had done a splendid thing. There was no denying it. But—

following a route close to the one that Peary had chosen for himself—
he'd crossed in the narrow southland. Peary now proposed to make a
much more daring and important trip. He'd cross far, far to the north.
His destination was to be the northeast corner of Greenland.

Why would such a crossing be important? Because, first, the lower
coasts of Greenland were well known. So were the northern reaches of
the west coast; long ago, explorers and whalers had made their way clear
up to Kane Basin. But the northeast corner—in all history, no one had
ever visited it. It was a blank spot on every map in the world. The first
man to go there and fill in the maps would perform an unforgettable
service for geography. And that man might also prove what geographers
had long suspected but never known for certain—that Greenland was a
vast island.

The chance to perform these services appealed to Peary on several
counts. For one, they would bring him even more fame than a southern
crossing. And they would certainly establish him as a leading Arctic
explorer. The problem of raising money for future expeditions would
disappear.

But, most important of all, the journey to the northeast corner might
well contribute to his ultimate goal—the conquest of the North Pole.
Perhaps the corner speared all the way up through the Arctic Ocean to
the Pole; or perhaps came close; or perhaps there were islands above it
that could be used as stepping-stones northward. Should any of these
prove true, Peary would have found what he called a "highway" to the
roof of the world.

With all this in mind, the explorer had planned his journey. He unrolled a map of Greenland. Come next June, he said, a chartered ship
would take them up to Inglefield Gulf. Once there, in late July, it would
put them ashore with their supplies and sail home to the United States.
They would winter at the Gulf, cross the icecap in the spring of next year,
and return in time to be picked up by the ship when it came back north to
fetch them.

Robert Peary pictured
in the furs that he wore
on his 1886 journey
to the Greenland icecap.

Matt nodded with excitement. But he had a question. Why spend the winter at Inglefield Gulf? Why not land and start the icecap journey at once?

The answer: thanks to the tilt of the earth, the Arctic year was roughly divided into two halves—one of daylight, the other of darkness. May, June, and July were the best months for crossing the cap because they gave the most daylight to travel by—twenty-four hours a day of it. But they were also the best months for sailing up Baffin Bay without running into ice pack so heavy that it would turn Peary's ship back.

And so he had no choice but to sail in one year and then camp at

Greenland through the winter—the season of darkness—and make the crossing as soon as there was enough light in the next year.

Further, once everything was ashore at Inglefield Gulf, time would be needed to prepare for the crossing. Peary said that Matt would see what he meant when they arrived.

Matt now learned that Peary had raised the money for the expedition by writing a detailed outline of what he planned to do. It hadn't brought a penny from the government because Washington wasn't presently interested in Arctic exploration. (And wouldn't be until well into the twentieth century.) But he'd sent it to several highly respected organizations, among them the American Geographical Society and the American Association for the Advancement of Science, and it had won their endorsement. This show of faith had prompted a number of scientific groups and wealthy individuals to finance the journey northward.

In the next weeks, working as both personal servant and assistant, Matt watched Peary put the finishing touches on his preparations. The explorer secured an eighteen-months' leave from the Navy; he'd expected an argument from his superiors over such a long absence, but they gave their approval because his Greenland findings might add some data to the Navy's coastal surveys. He ordered the last of his supplies. He chartered a Brooklyn-based ship. And, in April, he sent an announcement to several newspapers in various parts of the country. It outlined the journey and said that he was looking for "companions" to accompany him north.

As Peary had expected, the announcement brought a flood of letters and telegrams from young men—and some not so young—who yearned for adventure and were willing to challenge the Arctic. The most promising of the applicants were invited to Philadelphia for interviews. One after the other, Matt led them into Peary's office. Peary listened to them all, nodding as they spoke of their qualifications and hopes, and knowing the whole time that he was going to disappoint all but a mere four.

He planned to take the smallest number possible to Greenland—five men in all, including Matt. From his studies, he felt that a small party had a much better chance for success than a large one. Chiefly, it could move more swiftly and didn't have to be weighted down with so many supplies. Many early expeditions to the Arctic had ended in disaster. Peary was certain that they had brought on their own doom simply by carrying too many men.

The explorer made his selections by late May. The first nod went to Eivand Astrup, a twenty-one-year-old Norwegian. He was chosen not only for his strength and resistance to the cold but also because he had been a skiing champion back home. Skis were to be used on the expedition and Astrup would teach everyone how to get about on them.

Matt never forgot Peary's interview with Astrup. New to the United States, the young skier could speak little English and brought along an English-Norwegian dictionary as an aid. The intense way in which he leafed through the dictionary for needed words—plus what came out when he tried to pronounce them—finally got the better of Matt's sense of humor. Several times, Matt had to flee the room before bursting into laughter. Astrup later said that he had wondered why Matt kept disappearing through a side door with a "strange look" on his face. By then, they were good friends and a grinning Matt confessed the truth.

The second man chosen was bearded Dr. Frederick A. Cook, a surgeon from New York City. He was twenty-six years old and would serve as doctor to the expedition. He was also to help with an ethnological study that Peary hoped to make of the north Greenland Eskimos. It was one of several scientific works planned in addition to the crossing.

Peary had no inkling of it at the time, but he made one of the most fateful decisions of his life when he selected Cook. The doctor proved to be a genial companion and a fine worker, yes. But, in another twenty years, Peary would deeply regret ever having met him.

The explorer's final nods went to Langdon Gibson from Flushing, New York, and John Verhoeff of Kentucky. Both were in their middle twenties. Gibson, a member of the American Ornithologists' Society, would conduct a study of Greenland's wildlife. Verhoeff was to serve as mineralogist and meteorologist.

GIBSON.

VERHOEFF.

DR. COOK.

ASTRUP.

HENSON.

Matt and the four men chosen for the Greenland expedition of 1891–92.

Four applicants had been chosen, but to everyone's surprise, the party was to have yet another member. Peary announced that his wife Josephine would accompany him to Inglefield Gulf and remain there while he crossed the icecap. She had made it quite clear that she had no intention of being separated from her husband for more than a year. She'd had enough of loneliness during the Nicaraguan trip before their marriage.

Peary didn't argue. He had long ago written in his notebook that he

Peary's wife, Josephine.
Matt thought—correctly
—that she would do
well in the Arctic.

saw no reason why a woman shouldn't be part of an Arctic expedition. Further, he believed that a woman's grace and cheerfulness could do much to keep morale high.

At first, though saying nothing, Matt was troubled by the idea of a woman in the Arctic. But then he met Jo Peary and changed his mind. He found himself looking at a straight-backed young woman with level eyes and a firm chin. She came of a wealthy family and had been known as a belle of Washington society before her marriage, but there was nothing snobbish about her. Her smile was quick and her sense of humor good. Matt sensed in her an underlying strength that would serve her well in the Arctic—or in any place, for that matter. In the next months, and then the next years, he was to find out just how right he was.

Most of the country's newspapers, however, didn't share Matt's optimism. They were having a field day with the expedition, predicting that it was heading for disaster. They pointed out that a well-equipped expedition of two ships and 129 men under England's Sir John Franklin had disappeared among the frozen islands north of Canada in the 1840s. George Washington DeLong of the United States, just a dozen years ago, had lost more than half of his thirty-three men when the Arctic Ocean ice had crushed his ship during a voyage toward the Pole.

Now here was Peary planning to challenge the Greenland icecap with a small party of adventurers—and a woman, to boot.

He was mad. So was she. Man and wife were going to die.

Amid these gloomy predictions, the Peary group traveled to New York City at the end of May and went down to the East River, where their chartered ship lay at dock. Matt liked the look of the *Kite* immediately. She was a three-masted sealer with auxiliary steam. Small but sturdy— just 280 tons—she was captained by Richard Pike, an experienced Arctic seaman. She carried a crew of fifteen. To Matt, she seemed ready and eager for the sea.

So was he.

3. Greenland
1891-1892

Northward Bound

THE last boxes and parcels were finally stowed away on my little barkentine. At five in the afternoon of June 6, 1891, the *Kite* cast off from the foot of Baltic Street, Brooklyn, and swung out into the East River. Genial sunlight illuminated the faces of a crowd of friends and sightseers, waving adieus from the end of the pier. We were fairly off for North Greenland and every ferryboat and steamer in the East River knew it. Scores of whistles bade us good-bye and bon voyage . . ."

With these words, in his book *Northward Over the Great Ice*, Peary described the opening moments of the Greenland voyage. It was an exciting time for everyone on board. Matt watched a fleet of river steamers pass by, their passengers crowding the rails and waving handkerchiefs.

He couldn't help but wonder what all those well-wishers must be thinking. Surely, they must be asking themselves: how can such a small ship, so crowded and heavily loaded, ever hope to get where it's going?

He grinned to himself. In his time, he'd known some crowded conditions at sea. But never anything like this. Practically every inch of space above and below decks was crammed with equipment and supplies. On board was sufficient food to feed the party for a year and a half, plus—for safety's sake—enough coffee, tea, sugar, and condensed milk for another year. There were crates of evaporated vegetables. And crates of pemmican, the dried beef mixture that Peary would carry on the icecap. Nourishing and easily transported, it had been used by the Indians and pioneers back in America's early days.

The only thing in short supply was fresh meat. Peary intended to get all that was needed by shooting Arctic game.

Then there was the equipment. It ranged from skis and snowshoes to sledges and cooking utensils. And covering much of the deck were stacks of lumber. The wood was meant for the expedition's winter house at Inglefield Gulf. Matt's grin widened. Joining the wood on deck after a coming stop at Nova Scotia would be the tons of coal needed for burning through the Arctic winter.

Topping off everything were the people—thirty-one in all. In addition to the *Kite*'s crew of fifteen and Peary's party of seven, there were nine scientists on board. Headed by Professor Angelo Heilprin of Philadelphia's Academy of Natural Science, they planned to explore the Greenland coast during the time the supplies were being unloaded. They would then return home with the ship. Though they added much to the jam, Peary had consented to have them along because of a sizable financial contribution they had made to the expedition.

They proved to be nine very poor sailors after the *Kite* had made the coaling stop at Nova Scotia. In fact, practically all the passengers took dizzily to their bunks as the little ship nosed out of the Strait of Belle Isle and into some heavy Atlantic weather. The only exceptions were Matt and Peary. With mountainous waves on all sides, Matt became a seaman again and went aloft to help the crew shorten sail. Then he and Peary lent a hand with the pumps when tons of foaming water crashed in over the bows one afternoon and flooded the forward and waist compartments.

By June 23, the sea had quieted and all passengers were on deck for their first glimpse of what Peary called "the grandeur of Greenland." Late in the day, the rocky hulk of Cape Desolation loomed over the horizon. Within hours, the Greenland coast was stretching away to the north and south for as far as the eye could see.

The coast was as wild as Matt had expected it to be. Great shoulders of brownish rock and earth formed the shore. High above them, and in the great distance, the glittering white of the icecap could be glimpsed. Punctuating the tumbled brown of the shoreline were marblelike walls that sloped down from the heights to the sea. They were the great glaciers formed by the overflow of ice on the cap. The most breathtaking of all was the Frederikshaab Glacier. Peary told Matt that it was probably the largest one in the world.

In the next days, the *Kite* moved northward through Davis Strait and into Baffin Bay. Now Matt found himself surrounded by hundreds of icebergs, those great masses of blue-white that had broken away from the glaciers and floated out to sea. They were majestic sights never to be forgotten. Some were shaped like mountains. Two reminded Matt of giant ships. Some had been carved into arches and grottoes by the wind.

Once in Baffin Bay and with a course shaped through the summer's unending daylight for Inglefield Gulf, the *Kite* ran into heavy ice pack. Matt had seen floating ice ever since the Strait of Belle Isle, but now he was looking at a field of white that spread away in all directions. Its blinding surface was split with lanes of open water, called leads. The *Kite* pushed her way into these leads, always searching for the ones that speared northward.

But, often, the leads were too narrow for passage. And, often, there were no openings at all. Captain Pike would then put his ship into reverse. Then, with all the power that he could develop in the steam engine,

In Baffin Bay, Matt found himself surrounded by hundreds of icebergs. Some reminded him of giant ships.

he'd charge forward. Passengers and crew would grab anything for support as he rammed the bow into the ice. Sometimes, with a sound like a giant mirror cracking, the ice would part and grant him a few feet of forward progress. Sometimes, there would be a harsh grinding and an upward thrust and the bow would ride up on the ice, with its weight then splitting the ice and letting the ship drop forward. Everyone would relax —but only for a moment. Into reverse Pike would go for a fresh attack.

The pack slowed the progress north to just a few miles each day. And, on Saturday, July 11, it almost put an end to the expedition.

Matt was standing at the rail amidships as the *Kite* was battering her way through some particularly heavy ice. Peary joined him for a time and then moved aft to watch the two seamen at the wheel. In the moment that he arrived at the stern, a shudder went through the ship. Peary learned later that a huge cake of ice had smashed against the rudder and rammed

Heavy pack ice in Baffin Bay.

it sideways. The wheel spun out of the grasp of the two helmsmen. One sailor was thrown right over the hand grips and clear across the deck. The iron tiller running out from the wheel whipped from one side to the other. It scythed into Peary's right leg at the ankle. Crying out in sudden agony, he went down in a heap.

Matt turned just in time to see Peary fall. He rushed to the explorer. Through clenched teeth, Peary told him that he thought the leg was broken. One of the helmsmen went to fetch Dr. Cook. The doctor cut away Peary's boot and nodded grimly. The leg was indeed broken—badly, it seemed.

Matt and Langdon Gibson carried the explorer to his cabin and placed him on his bunk. Dr. Cook set the leg and then told Peary just how serious the injury was. Both bones in the lower leg were broken, snapped off just above the ankle. Long weeks would be needed for the breaks to mend. Long weeks of pain.

Cook looked straight at the explorer. Peary, he said, couldn't possibly think of camping at Inglefield Gulf for the winter. He'd never be able to move about on the rough shore. And, come spring, he could never expect to cross the icecap—a round-trip journey of an estimated 1,200 miles.

The doctor said that Peary had just one choice. He had to turn for home.

2.

Give up?

Peary wouldn't hear of it. Nothing was going to keep him from his goal. He wasn't going to disappoint his financial backers. Nor was he going to give the newspapers—all those papers that had been predicting disaster—the chance to accuse him of quitting at the first sign of trouble. If he retreated now, he'd be ruined as an explorer.

Cook tried to argue, but Peary waved him down. The trip across the icecap lay almost ten months away. He was sure that he'd be fit by then. In the meantime, he'd survive. Everyone could bet on *that*!

But Matt wondered if the explorer really could handle the rigors of the coming Arctic winter. He saw Peary's face tighten with pain every time the plunging *Kite* slammed into the ice. How would the leg ever stand the winter cold? How would Peary ever manage to start walking again over on that rough Greenland shore?

With the leg splinted in a narrow wooden box that Matt built, Peary remained a prisoner in his cabin for the rest of the voyage. Matt and Jo Peary could see how difficult things were for her husband. The pain itself was bad enough. But worse was the fact that Peary could not take part in the exciting life all about him. Whenever there was a burst of voices on the deck outside, he would straighten and demand to know what was going on.

Then either Matt or Jo would climb up on a bunk and, peering through the cabin skylight, report that a giant iceberg was looming in the distance. Or that a walrus had poked its head out of an opening in the ice pack. One morning, a polar bear was sighted less than a hundred yards from the ship. Eleven rifles all opened fire in the same instant. Minutes later, Jo was telling her husband of how the body of the animal—all 600 pounds of it—was being hauled aboard with ropes.

On another morning, a polar bear and her two cubs ambled by. They were just out of rifle range. Professor Heilprin and his scientists clamored over the side with their rifles to give chase. One hunter was so excited that he was down on the ice and running hard before he realized that he'd forgotten to bring his rifle. The mother and cubs easily outdistanced their pursuers.

Matt and Jo couldn't help but smile at the embarrassment of the forgetful hunter. Soon, they had another reason to smile, this time in relief. As the *Kite* moved past Cape York and neared Inglefield Gulf, she broke out of the ice pack and into a stretch of clear water. Smoothly and quickly, the little ship moved through a calm sea. Peary was left free of pain for the first time in days.

There was a moment of disappointment, though, when the *Kite* arrived at Inglefield Gulf. Ice that had come down from the glaciers at its far end choked the gulf, making it impossible to land and end the journey there. Peary checked his maps and ordered the ship to McCormick Bay, a narrow inlet just to the north. Should it be free of ice, his party would winter there. And, spearing inland for fifteen miles as it did, the bay would serve as well as the Gulf as a jumping-off spot for the icecap march.

The *Kite* swung into McCormick Bay the next morning. There were ice floes everywhere, but not enough of them to prevent a landing. To the north and south sides of the bay entrance stood blunt points of land. The point on the south side caught and held everyone's eye. Alive with wildflowers, it ran gently up from a rocky shore to the base of a high red cliff.

Peary immediately put his people to the first of their Arctic jobs. He sent them out in two whaleboats—one to the northern shore, the other to the southern side—to find the best site possible for their winter house. Accompanied by Matt, Jo rode to the southern side and stepped ashore.

The search lasted throughout the day, and it was Jo who found the best site. She chose a small knoll near the base of the red cliff. The land there fell gently away on all sides, promising good drainage during the winter storms. The earth underfoot was soft. The job of digging out a level space for the house would be fairly easy.

Once the site was selected, four busy days of work followed. On Sunday, July 26, Peary's men—or, as he always called them, "the boys" —began leveling the ground. Professor Heilprin and his friends explored along the shores. The *Kite*'s crew got to the job of unloading the ship.

Floating ice made it impossible for the *Kite* to lie at anchor during the unloading; there was too much danger of jagged-edged floes slamming into her and ripping her hull. And so she steamed slowly back and forth while all the supplies for the expedition were passed from the deck to small boats and then rowed over to the shore. From there, the supplies were manhandled up to the site of the house.

Moved in this fashion were several hundred supply boxes, all the lumber for the house, and just over 100 tons of coal.

The lumber went ashore first so that it would be right at hand as soon as the level spot was dug out. The digging was finished in one day, by Monday, July 27. Shovels were dropped and hammers picked up in their place. On that same day, Peary came ashore.

Rather, he was brought ashore. To make the job easier, Matt strapped him securely to a long plank. Then the explorer was carried up to the deck, lifted over the side, and lowered to a waiting boat. None of the watchers dared to breathe. One slip and Peary would end up in the icy water. Matt stood ready to dive over the side in an instant.

But there was no slip. In another thirty minutes, Peary was safely ashore and seated in the opening of a tent that had been erected up on the leveled knoll. From here, with his broken leg stretched out in front of him, he would supervise the construction of the winter house.

Matt saw Peary look about with pleasure. There was no doubt about

Members of the expedition posed for a photograph in front of their winter quarters as soon as Red Cliff House was completed. Matt is at the far left, with Jo Peary next to him. Peary, resting his broken leg, sits on a packing crate at right.

it; Jo had picked a lovely spot. Two little streams ran close-by, one to either side of the knoll. Directly below, the ice in McCormick Bay sparkled under the Arctic sun. Peary caught his breath. There, breaking the surface just beyond the *Kite*, was a school of white whales.

Soon, the winter house was pleasing the explorer just as much as his surroundings. Careful and thorough as always, he had planned it right down to the last detail back in Philadelphia. Then, during the voyage north, his boys had precut its lumber to exact size. Now, to the unending rattle of hammers, the place was taking shape with amazing speed.

When finished, its interior would measure 21 feet long, 12 feet wide, and 8 feet from floor to ceiling. It was to be divided into two rooms—a small private bedroom for Jo and himself, and a large room where the cooking and winter work would be done and where the boys would sleep.

As Peary had planned it, the outer sides of the house would be constructed of closely fitting boards and two layers of tar paper. Likewise, closely fitting boards would be used for the inner walls. To seal out every last bit of wind, brown paper would be pasted over all the inner-wall joints. Then the inner walls would be draped with red Indian blankets.

Matt grinned to himself whenever he thought of those blankets. It was certainly going to be a colorful place.

By Tuesday, July 28, all supplies were at the knoll. It was time for the *Kite* to head for home. After taking aboard letters from the party to loved ones back in the States, she sounded her whistle in farewell and moved slowly out of McCormick Bay. Left behind for the winter were seven Americans with their tons of supplies and two whaleboats. The *Kite* was scheduled to return in exactly a year. By that time—if all went well—Peary would have crossed Greenland and found her northeastern shores.

3.

If his people were at all saddened by the *Kite*'s departure, they gave no sign of it. Back to their hammers they went. Work on the house—interrupted once by a sudden storm that almost blew Matt off the rafters as he was helping to put the roof on—progressed so well that the place was ready for occupancy by August 11. Bunks for the boys were ranged round the walls of the main room. Tables, chairs, and a potbellied stove were brought in. A bookcase made of a packing box was set up. Peary looked about with satisfaction and announced that the house must now have a name—Red Cliff House in honor of the cliff that loomed above it.

Though the house itself was complete, further work remained to be done on the winter quarters. Peary's supplies had been carried north in boxes all of the same size. He had ordered them built this way so that they could now be fashioned into a four-foot-high wall that was to run all around the outside of the house. Once the wall was in place three feet out from the house, a canvas sheet would be stretched from the uppermost boxes to the roof. Formed would be a covered corridor. With the coal stacked in the corridor, anyone could step outside to fetch some fuel or open a supply box without being blasted by the fierce winter winds.

The job of building the wall fell to Matt because Peary had another assignment for the rest of his boys. As the explorer had said back in Philadelphia, many preparations for the crossing would have to be made once everyone was ashore at Greenland. He now began those preparations by having the boys sail one of the whaleboats south toward Inglefield Gulf. With Cook in charge, they were to locate the Eskimos living thereabouts and induce them and their families to come and live alongside Red Cliff House for the winter.

From the very beginning, Peary had planned to have the Eskimos work for him. He wanted the men to hunt and supply the expedition with fresh meat. The women were to sew the hides of the downed animals into clothing for the icecap trip; Peary had long ago learned from his studies —and from his 1886 Greenland visit—that the animal-skin outfits worn by the Eskimos had the woolens of civilization beaten hands-down when it came to protecting a man against the terrible cold. Finally, the Eskimos were to provide him with hardy Arctic dogs to pull his sledges on the crossing. He planned to pay the Eskimos for their services and animals with food, rifles, ammunition, and household goods.

Though not knowing a word of Eskimo, the four men departed on August 12. The next days passed quietly at Red Cliff House. Matt worked on the wall of supply boxes. Jo planned and cooked the daily meals. Peary began to exercise his broken leg back into shape. He could stand on it now, though only with much pain, and he spent some time each day hobbling about on crutches that Matt had fashioned.

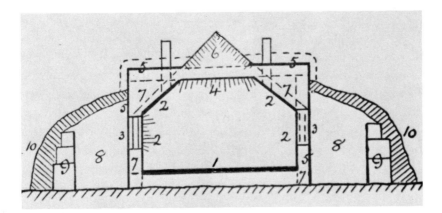

1. Double floor, with tarred paper between
2. Inner sheathing, lined with blankets or felt
3. Double windows
4. Overhead sash to prolong Arctic day
5. Outer sheathing, with tarred paper inside and out; outer joints covered with battens
6. Lantern or skylight
7. Air spaces between inner and outer sheathing, from 1 to 3 feet wide
8. Corridors, 5 to 6 feet wide, 6 to 7 feet high, extending entirely around house for protection from cold and as storehouses
9. Walls formed of supply boxes, enclosing the corridors
10. Snow embankments, blanketing corridors, and roof

Peary's general plan for an Arctic dwelling. Red Cliff House was based on this plan.

On the morning of August 18, Matt dashed into the Pearys' bedroom. He said that he had just sighted the returning whaleboat. Peary, hurrying as best he could, made his way to the shore in time to greet the boat when it landed. He was delighted to see that his boys were not alone. In the whaleboat with them were four Eskimos—a man, a woman, and two children.

Dr. Cook performed the introductions. The man's name, he said, was Ikwa. The woman was Mane, his wife. Their children—a little girl of about four and an infant—were Annadore and Noya.

Peary listened intently as Cook explained how he'd sighted a couple of Eskimo camps near the Gulf, but had found them deserted. Then he had met the family wandering along a shore three days ago. Using sign language, he'd talked Ikwa into coming along to Red Cliff House, where there was work and food. Peary saw the man's harpoon, sledge, and dog in the boat. A kayak bobbed at the end of a rope off the stern.

Smiling, Ikwa and Mane shook hands with Peary. They had seen white men before—the whalers who visited Greenland waters—and so they weren't awestruck by Peary or the whaleboat crew. But then they sighted Jo. Their eyes widened. Here was a totally alien creature. A white woman, with her hair not falling naturally to her shoulders but piled into a mountain on top of her head. And wearing a strange garment that fell all the way to the ground and gave her the appearance of having no legs or feet.

While Jo stood there patiently, Ikwa and Mane circled her, chattering to each other and—if their giggles and then their laughter were to be believed—finding her the most hilarious spectacle that they had ever seen. In time, Jo was to learn that they meant her no insult. It was just that they were simple people who had never mastered the art of hiding their feelings.

But, suddenly, Ikwa had no more time for Jo. He had glimpsed Matt standing nearby. His eyes widened even more. His smile was broader than ever. He threw his arms out wide and ran to Matt.

An astonished Matt found himself caught in an embrace of animal furs. An odor that was part human, part reindeer, and part walrus enveloped him. He heard the man shouting close to his ear. Ikwa was saying a strange word over and over again. It sounded like "Innuit." Yes. That was it. "Innuit."

In his confusion, Matt fell back a step. Ikwa's leathery face came into view. Again, there was that word—"Innuit." With a helpless shrug, Matt got the idea across that he did not understand. Ikwa thought for a moment, then suddenly pulled back the sleeve of his animal-skin coat, held his dark arm alongside Matt's equally dark hand, and pointed from one to the other. And, just as suddenly, Matt *did* understand. Ikwa took him for a fellow Eskimo, come from a distant place to work with the white men. "Innuit." That must mean Eskimo in Ikwa's language.

Matt now shook his head. He tried to sign that, though he was dark, he was not an Innuit. But, as he was to find with all the Eskimos who came to live at Red Cliff House, he was wasting his time. They had seen white men before and, in their uncomplicated view, all people were divided into two kinds—white and dark. All dark people were Eskimos. Matt was an Eskimo.

Matt did not realize it as he stood there staring at Ikwa's blunt features and dark eyes, but a world of new friendships was opening up to him at that moment. For as long as he worked in the Arctic, all the Eskimos whom he met were to look on him as a brother who had been born in a faraway land. They taught him to speak their language, to eat their food, and to live as they did. For his part, he responded with affection and proved to be an apt pupil. In time, he became as adept as they in the art of surviving in the Arctic wastes.

His willingness to learn and his affection for them soon won him a special name among the Eskimos. To Ikwa and all the others, after this warmest of welcomes to Greenland, he became "Miy Paluk." It meant "dear little Matthew."

4. Greenland
1891-1892

Assault on the Icecap

SOMEHOW, the news that Ikwa and his family were at Peary's camp spread to the other Eskimos in the area. Soon, several families sledged in to join the expedition. By the time winter arrived in October, there was a small settlement of stone and ice huts circling Red Cliff House.

Matt could see that Peary was pleased with the way things were going. The construction of the winter house and the arrival of the Eskimos meant that two vital jobs had been completed. The explorer turned to the next of his preparations. A good route had to be found up to the icecap. Then supplies for the crossing had to be taken up and stored near the cap.

These jobs needed to be done before the winter tied everyone down to

Red Cliff House. Once spring dawned, Peary would have just so many weeks to make the crossing and return in time to be picked up by the *Kite*. He dared not keep the ship waiting for fear that she might not get away before the bad weather came again. And so no spring days could be wasted searching for a route to the cap and then hauling up the many necessary supplies.

On August 31, Peary sent Eivand Astrup off to the far end of Mc-Cormick Bay—fifteen miles in the distance—to see if it offered any kind of access to the cap. Astrup returned in sixteen hours. He reported that the bay terminated at a valley. There were bluffs above the valley and then land sloping upwards above them. They were rugged-looking slopes, but Astrup felt that they could be climbed to the cap without too much trouble.

Ikwa signed that the valley was a good hunting area, alive with reindeer; in fact, it bore the Eskimo word for reindeer—tooktoo. A few days later, Peary filled the whaleboat with supplies and rode to the valley with Astrup, Langdon Gibson, and John Verhoeff. He left them there with instructions to find a good path upwards and then lay in a supply depot as close to the cap as possible. While they were on this assignment, he said, he planned to take the whaleboat down to Inglefield Gulf in search of more Eskimos for the Red Cliff settlement.

It was a trip that lasted more than a week and netted not a single glimpse of an Eskimo. But it was a trip that almost ended in disaster for the explorer and his companions—Matt, Jo, Dr. Cook, and Ikwa. The Eskimo was along as both guide and interpreter.

The trouble began when the whaleboat cut her way into a school of walrus. Startled gray heads—looking like giant, creased rocks—broke the surface of the water on all sides. There was the flash of whitish tusks. Then an angry snorting sound. And then the disturbed water was being churned to an icy foam.

Ikwa was the first to recognize the danger. He'd seen this happen before. Led by an enraged bull, the walrus were going to attack the boat.

The Eskimo screamed a warning and jumped to the bow. He grabbed his harpoon. In the next instant, he was beating it against the bulwarks to the accompaniment of a screeching yell that went on and on—his native way of driving off the charging animals.

Matt, Cook, and Peary all moved at the same time. Repeating rifles came swinging up. Shot after shot pounded into the water and into the crashing gray hides. Blood appeared on the surface. Tusks flashed just inches away from the boat—tusks that would have torn right through the boards had they reached their mark. Matt emptied his first magazine. A giant head loomed close; he smacked the rifle barrel down hard on it; the walrus dove beneath the boat. Matt spent an agonizing moment waiting for the thing to come straight up under him and pitch the whole crew into the sea. The moment passed. He began reloading.

Then, out of the corner of his eye, he saw Jo crawling along the floorboards. She was making her way to Peary in the stern. She positioned herself so that her body shielded her husband's broken leg from a collision with Matt and Cook as they swung to fire from side to side. Then she was handing up spare rifles to the men and reloading the empty ones that they passed to her. After that, there wasn't a single break in the firing.

The attack ended as abruptly as it had begun. With at least four of their number dead, the walrus suddenly turned away. Moments later, the sea was calm again, and the air quiet.

On returning to Red Cliff House, Peary found Astrup and his two helpers already there. The young Norwegian, his face gaunt with exhaustion, said that he had some bad news. He still felt that the icecap could be reached fairly easily from the bluffs in good weather, but his party had run into a storm up there. It had whipped them mercilessly and had frozen Verhoeff's face. In two tries, they hadn't been able to establish a supply depot.

Matt saw Peary's face tighten. The news was bad indeed. It was now late September and winter would arrive in early October. There was no time left to try again for a depot. This meant that the expedition would have to work doubly hard at the first signs of spring. Unless the supplies were quickly placed at that time, Peary would never reach his goal and get back before the *Kite* arrived.

With troubled eyes, Matt watched the sun end its restless circling of the Greenland sky in October. After dipping lower and lower each day— and turning a duller and duller red as it did so—it disappeared below the horizon. Now there would be a deepening twilight for a time. Then a night darkness would lay for weeks on Red Cliff House, a darkness that would divide itself between howling storms and weather so clear that the moonlight would polish the ice in McCormick Bay to a glowing blue-white.

In February, the sun would appear again, but only for a few moments on the first day of its rising. Then, little by little, it would daily push itself higher above the horizon until, by next May, it would again be circling the sky twenty-four hours a day and Peary would be heading northeast.

But heading northeast only if the supplies could be gotten up to the cap quickly enough. Matt felt something that he hadn't even felt when the tiller had smashed into Peary's leg back on the *Kite*.

He felt that the expedition was looking failure right in the face.

2.

Any misgivings about the supply problem did not keep the people at Red Cliff House from having a busy winter. Daily, John Verhoeff made meteorological observations and searched for mineral specimens down by McCormick Bay. When the sky was clear, Astrup prepared the explorers for the springtime journey by teaching them to ski. Matt hunted with Ikwa and assisted Jo with the cooking.

As for Peary, he and Dr. Cook launched their ethnological studies of the Eskimos. All newly arriving families were invited into the house, first to have their body measurements taken and then to be photographed. In all, seventy-five Eskimos were measured and photographed.

So that their body structures could be studied by researchers back home, Peary asked the Eskimos to pose for his camera with all their clothes off, except for the loin cloths they wore. The request puzzled them and they balked at the idea until the explorer, with Ikwa interpreting, managed to explain that he needed the pictures to compare Eskimo bodies with those of other people in the world. Then they willingly did as he asked.

He later learned that, at first, they had suspected that he wanted to use the pictures and measurements for the purpose of making new people.

In addition to his picture-taking, Peary made endless notes on the life and customs of the Eskimos. He found that they belonged to a small tribe of about 250 men, women, and children. They were sprinkled throughout the coastal area between Cape York on the south and Kane Basin on the north. Peary called them the most northerly people on earth.

They lived in complete isolation from the rest of the world. There was a Mongolian cast to their features and an Oriental touch to their manner. Peary knew that an anthropological theory of the day held that their ancestors had lived in Siberia and, after being driven out by the Tartar invasions of the Middle Ages, had wandered into the Arctic wastes. He thought that the look of the people around him gave much credence to the theory.

Their environment was savage and hostile. They lived the most primitive life imaginable. Peary noted that they had no government, no money, no religion (but a welter of superstitions), no written language, and no personal property except their clothing, sledges, dogs, weapons, and a few household utensils. Their diet consisted of nothing but meat, blood, and blubber; salt and vegetables were unknown to them. Their clothes were made of the skins of animals and birds. Their main goals in life were to find food and the materials for clothing.

But, though poor in physical goods, they were rich in other things. Peary found them hardy, strong, and impervious to the cold. He wrote that they were intelligent, resourceful, and full of good humor. They laughed quickly and frequently. They took pleasure in each other's company. They enjoyed sports such as foot racing, tumbling, and thumb wrestling. And they were fascinated by all the strange equipment that Peary had brought into their midst.

Of all the equipment, one item seemed to fascinate them the most—Peary's flashlight. They couldn't get over the fact that it never failed to erupt in dazzling light at the touch of a finger. Peary used the flashlight to provide illumination for the photographs, and every newcomer heard about it from his friends as soon as he arrived at Red Cliff House. Then, after he had stood in its glare while his picture was taken, he invariably told the whole camp of his adventure. Not a detail was spared. Matt remarked that the listeners never seemed to tire of hearing essentially the same story from every new arrival.

While Peary took his pictures and made his notes, Jo sat close-by with two Eskimo women and a young girl. Working together, the foursome cut out and then stitched together the animal-skin clothes, boots, and sleeping bags that the icecap party would need come spring. Used were the skins of several Eskimo dogs that had died, and of sixteen reindeer that had been shot for food. Matt and Ikwa had downed nine of the reindeer on a trip to Tooktoo Valley.

The work of preparing the skins for sewing required the utmost patience. Once each skin had been dried, it needed to be softened so that it could be worn with comfort. The softening was accomplished in the most primitive of ways—by chewing.

To start, an Eskimo woman folded the skin with the hair inside. Then she chewed her way back and forth along the fold until the material became pliable. A new fold was made an inch or so away and the chewing began afresh, with the process continuing until the whole skin was done. Final softening came when the skin was scraped with a blunt instrument made of animal bone. If this last procedure didn't finish things off, the skin was chewed once more. Peary wrote that it took the Eskimo women two days to chew a single large skin.

If the Eskimo women were busy with Jo, their husbands were even busier with Peary and his boys. They taught the visitors their language, a language that contained well over 3,000 words. They taught them how to fashion igloos of blocks cut from the ice. They taught them how to hunt Eskimo-style. And they taught them how to drive a sledge and its team of Arctic dogs.

For as long as he lived, Matt never forgot his first driving lesson. To begin with, he was fascinated by the Eskimo sledge and the dog team. The sledge itself was about twelve feet long and built low to the ground, with the runners often made of walrus tusks. At its rear end were two upright handles, which the Americans called upstanders. The driver did not ride on the sledge. Rather, he ran behind it and guided it by grasping the upstanders, much as a farmer guides a plow.

As for the dogs, they were the sharp-nosed descendants of the Arctic white wolf. They were to be seen in a variety of markings and in colors that ranged from yellow to coal black. Their coats were a thick but shabby-looking fur. Their tails were bushy. Matt soon came to look upon these animals with great respect. He was sure that they could work harder and longer on less food than any other animal in the world.

Eight dogs were needed to pull a sledge carrying an average load of supplies. The animals were placed alongside each other, and each was fitted into a trace of its own. The traces, which were about fourteen feet long, all ran back to a harness at the front of the sledge. When the dogs pulled the sledge, they spread out into a fanlike formation.

At the forefront of the fan was the king dog, the team leader. When a team was first formed, the dogs all fought each other for the position of leader, with the prize going to the strongest and fiercest of the lot. Once the king dog was chosen, the other members of the team would follow him anywhere without question, going wherever he went, no matter how great the smell of danger seemed to be. Whenever any new dogs joined the team, the leader had to defend his job by fighting and defeating them.

Ikwa and his good friend of many years—Ahnalka—gave Matt his

The dogs in harness, waiting for Matt to take his first lesson in sledge driving.

first lessons in sledging. They took him to a level spot below the knoll and showed him how a driver urged the team along with shouts of "Huk! Huk!" and the snap of a whip. The whip, some thirty feet long and made of seal rawhide, was a vicious-looking thing, but Matt learned immediately that it was always wielded with great delicacy. No dog was ever flayed with it.

Rather, if a dog misbehaved or tried to pull away in a direction all his own, the whip went curling out and snapped with the sound of a gunshot just above his ear. Ikwa said that the dog immediately became a good dog again—not because he had been hurt but because that exploding whip promised that there would be pain if he didn't change his ways.

Ikwa demonstrated how the whip was snapped; it was done with a forward motion of the elbow, followed by a strong flick of the wrist. Then he handed the whip to Matt, stationed him at the upstanders, and stood aside with Ahnalka to see what would happen. In a moment, the two Eskimos were grinning. In another, they were collapsing against each other in roaring laughter.

Matt began with that strange shout, "Huk! Huk!" but nothing happened. The dogs had no intention of moving forward at the sound of an

Matt developed a great respect for the Eskimo sledge dogs. He was sure that they could work longer and harder on less food than any other animal in the world.

unfamiliar voice. They looked back over their shoulders, glimpsed the stranger, appeared to shrug, and went down on their haunches to await the return of someone they knew. Matt decided to try the whip. He sent it sailing harmlessly—and silently—above the king dog's head.

He tried again. The tip arced it way off to the left and puffed up the snow near Ikwa's feet. Another try: a convulsed Ahnalka darted for safety as Ikwa was nicked high on the shoulder. A final attempt, this time a half-angry one: somehow, the rawhide came snaking back and wrapped itself around Matt's legs, unceremoniously dumping him over on his backside. He looked at his Eskimo teachers. As far as he could tell, he was the comic highlight of their winter.

Their laughter, however, turned into proud smiles in the next weeks. Thanks to some daily practice out behind the house, Matt was soon handling the whip with a good beginning skill. By the end of December, he could move a team by himself. When spring dawned, he was easily the best driver among the Americans, and Ikwa was saying that this Innuit from faraway would soon be as adept as his brothers here in the north.

3.

That first lesson in sledging was just one of the many adventures that punctuated the winter work of the expedition. The Arctic night brought plunging temperatures and a series of raging storms. One of the worst lashed Red Cliff House on New Year's Eve. In the course of just one night, it almost buried the place in snow.

But the storm failed to interfere with the party given by the Pearys to welcome 1892. Right from the start, the couple had decided to celebrate all holidays and special occasions; it would help to keep morale high. Back in August, there had been festive dinners on Matt's twenty-fifth birthday and on the Pearys' third wedding anniversary. Thanksgiving and Christmas had been observed, the latter with a dinner for some of the Eskimos. Now, on December 31, as the wind screamed outside, Jo presided over a late evening snack of cookies, doughnuts, and ice cream. She wore a black-and-yellow tea gown that had been carefully packed away in her trunk. At midnight, seven glasses of wine were raised in a toast to the new year—and to the great springtime journey.

A few days later, there was a moment of adventure that could have ended in tragedy but that turned, instead, into a good laugh at Dr. Cook's expense. It happened when Astrup accidentally knocked a large and open box of matches from a shelf.

The matches struck the hot stove, immediately ignited, and bounced away in all directions. Cook, who had been dozing in his bunk, popped awake. He threw himself at the flames, landing on all fours just in time to take a pail of water full in the face from Peary. A second pailful came from Matt. Another from Peary extinguished the fire. The water had been kept close at hand for just such an emergency and, as a chilled Cook toweled himself dry, Matt grinned that the doctor had to admit one

The interior of Red Cliff House. When a box of matches accidentally fell on the stove in the foreground and burst into flames, the "Red Cliff Fire Department" went into action.

thing—the "Red Cliff Fire Department" had performed with admirable efficiency.

The greatest adventure of all got underway when spring dawned in February and March. With the sun returning and rising a little higher each day, the final preparations for the crossing began. The supplies were assembled and Peary's men spent the weeks into April hurrying them up to the bluffs above Tooktoo Valley. He himself sledged over to Inglefield Gulf in search of Eskimos who would sell him the remaining dogs needed for the journey. He had nine in camp already and wanted a total of twenty. He came back with eleven.

On April 30, Cook went to the Valley with a final load of supplies, taking Astrup, Gibson, and five Eskimos with him. Three days later, a relieved Peary left Red Cliff House for the last time; thanks to some very hard work, all the supplies had been quickly put into place and he had ample time for the crossing. Accompanied by Matt, he sledged out to join Cook.

In the moments just before leaving, the explorer kissed Jo good-bye and promised to return safely. Then, at his sledge, he paused to smile up at a small flag flying above it at the end of a slender pole. Sewn by Jo, it was a guidon made of a silk handkerchief emblazoned with a blue star cut from one of her tea gowns. Wherever Peary went on the icecap— whether in driving snows or icy fogs—it would enable his men to keep track of his sledge.

4.

One thought filled Matt's head on the run to the Valley. He knew that Peary did not intend to take all his boys across the icecap; they would require too many supplies. Rather, their job was to get supplies up to the cap for him. Then he would choose two companions for the crossing. They would be the most competent and least tired of the group. Matt hoped that he would be one of the two picked.

He realized that his chances were slim. He'd spent the winter mainly tending to the needs of the Pearys and he knew that the explorer really viewed him more as a servant than a full-fledged member of the expedition. But Matt had early set out to prove himself as good an Arctic hand as he had been a chainman in Nicaragua. He had learned to build a good igloo and had become the best sledger in the group. Surely, Peary would recognize his worth and point to him when the time came.

On reaching the Valley, Matt and Peary climbed immediately to Cook on the bluffs. The doctor reported that, from here, his party had worked their way up toward the icecap for a distance of two and a half miles. There, at an altitude of 2,500 feet, they had established what they called Cache Camp. They were just now starting to sledge supplies up to it.

Later, the supplies would be moved the remaining few miles to the cap itself.

Matt quickly pitched in to help with the work of stocking Cache Camp, a job that took two days. He manhandled his dogs and heavily laden sledge up a steep incline and then along a glacier. The incline was splashed with jagged ice and rocks that ripped his animal-skin boots. On the glacier, he felt a strange hollowness underfoot at times and knew that he was crossing deep crevasses that were hidden beneath the snow. All the while, high winds and snow squalls beat at him. On reaching the camp, he joined Astrup in building an igloo to shelter the men climbing up behind them. Then he ran into heartbreaking disappointment.

It came when he returned to the bluffs for another load. He was limping with an aching pain in the heel of one foot. Peary asked about the limp and summoned Cook, and the doctor put an end to Matt's hopes of crossing the icecap. The heel was badly frozen. Cook felt it would be too dangerous for Matt to continue; he should return to Red Cliff House.

Peary saw the disappointment in the black man's face. The explorer said that he would feel better with Matt back at the house. He asked him to keep an eye on Jo and—in the event that the crossing ended in death somewhere up there on the cap—to see that she got safely home. Matt nodded. It would be a poor substitute for the adventure of the crossing, but he would do as Peary asked.

Matt returned to Red Cliff House, arriving on May 7, and found that he had a troubled Jo on his hands. She had always been secretly worried about her husband's journey. First, even though he'd ventured onto the cap back in 1886, he was anything but an experienced Arctic traveler as yet; anything could happen to him. And there was his leg. The break was healed, yes, but he was still in pain. He usually walked with clenched teeth and, just a few days before his departure, she had seen the leg swell up to three times its normal size after a strenuous hike. Now that he was on his way, the chances of disaster seemed overwhelming to her.

Cook and his party—with the exception of Astrup—appeared at the house on May 30. Cook said that all the supplies had been sledged onto the cap by May 24. At that time, Peary had decided that, in the interests of speed, he would make the crossing with just one man instead of the planned two. He had selected the muscular Astrup as his companion and had sent the others home.

Dr. Cook's story of the move up onto the icecap did nothing to allay Jo's fears. The party, he said, had endured some terrible hardships. A fierce storm had delayed them for twenty-four hours at one point. Another time, a howling wind had lifted several supply crates from alongside a sledge and had hurled them down a slope to a glacier far below. They had barely missed Peary as they had whirled away.

The doctor tried to comfort Jo with the assurance that the weather had changed for the better by the time Peary and Astrup had departed with their sledges. And the surface had been smooth. Peary had been on snowshoes, and Astrup on skis. They would make a swift and safe crossing. She could count on it.

But Jo refused to be consoled. Her worry persisted through June and July, deepening all the while. She tried to occupy her mind with housework, cooking, and long walks along the shore with Matt. But nothing helped. Making matters worse was an Eskimo named Kyo. He insisted that he had magical powers and delighted in telling Jo of visions that he saw while in a trance. They were always of a lone white man fighting his way home across the icecap. The man, he said, was not Peary.

By late July, the woman could no longer stand the strain. With Matt, she went up to Tooktoo Valley and made camp, there to await her husband's return. Word reached her a few days later that the *Kite* had arrived off Red Cliff House. In yet another few days, Professor Heilprin hiked in to stay at the camp.

The first day of August came and went. Though Peary had expected to be back by this time, he had cautioned Jo not to be upset should he be a few days late. But, by now, she had no memory for his confident words. Her worry had turned to a sick fear. All that she could think was that her husband was overdue. Something had happened to him.

Professor Heilprin shared her fears. He organized a search party and started for the icecap on August 5. Early the next morning, he came upon Peary and Astrup as they were moving down the glacier above the cliffs. He stared at the two men. They looked as if they had been in a battle. Their faces were gaunt with exhaustion and their eyes bloodshot from snow blindness. Their boots were in shreds, their sledges battered, and the feet of their remaining dogs so lacerated that the animals could barely walk.

But none of this seemed to matter to the two explorers. They staggered to Heilprin and shook his hand and he knew immediately that their journey had been a magnificent success. A short time later, Peary was embracing the relieved Jo. She was so happy that she hardly heard his words—the proud news that he had marched clear across Greenland and back.

5.

In the warmth of Red Cliff House a few days later, a rested Peary looked at the circle of eager faces and, with Astrup, told the story of the crossing.

Their first days of travel, Peary said, had been good, with smooth ice underfoot. But they had ended May in an area of snow so thick and deep that the dogs refused to work and had to be grasped and pulled ahead. In June, there was a snowstorm that pinned them down for two days. And a nightmare region of yawning crevasses that had to be skirted. And a slippery downhill grade that sent the sledges fishtailing and caused the men and dogs to take a number of bad falls.

But, by early July, the explorers came off the far side of the icecap. They sighted mountains looming in the distance to the north and east and headed for them. Once, in a valley of brown earth, they paused for several hours to rest and to feast on two musk oxen that they shot; neither could remember when last they and the dogs had eaten fresh meat. Then, as they were threading their way among some sharp rocks, with the mountains drawing steadily nearer, they stopped again—this time suddenly. This time, to stare in wonder at the scene before them.

Navy Cliff loomed high above Independence Bay at the northeastern corner of Greenland.

They had been crossing a plateau and, without warning, had come to the brink of a giant cliff. From the tips of their feet, it dropped 4,000 feet to a vast bay that spread away into the mists. Widening as it went, the bay stretched north and east into what seemed to be the Arctic Ocean. It also ran westward; Peary stared into the great distance and thought that he saw where this westward arm, too, opened into the Arctic Ocean. Northward, beyond the bay, were the mountains. Peary guessed that they were the crowns of offshore islands.

If all this were true—if the bay opened into the Arctic Ocean on the west and northeast and if the mountainous lands to the north were islands—then he had done what he had come north to do. He had reached the northeastern corner of Greenland.

Peary christened the water Independence Bay, in honor of the day of its discovery—July 4. To the cliff on which he stood went the name Navy Cliff. Off to his right, an enormous glacier was flowing into the bay; he called it Academy Glacier, for the Naval Academy at Annapolis. The mountainous lands across the water were given various names, among them Heilprin Land for Professor Heilprin, and Daly Land for Judge Charles P. Daly, the president of the American Geographical Society.

Peary wished that he could explore the area, but he dared not linger here. His supplies were running low and the date for the *Kite*'s arrival in McCormick Bay was fast approaching. He must return to Red Cliff House at once. On July 5, he and Astrup built a rock cairn on Navy Cliff, placed a written record of their discovery in it, and turned their faces west.

The homeward march proved to be as difficult as the one outbound. Storms dogged the two men. Rough ice damaged their sledges. Both men, after staring into a cold white world for too long, had to contend with snow blindness. On July 17, Peary scribbled in his notebook that his eyes were "almost useless."

But they had survived the ordeal and, just one month after departing Navy Cliff, had come upon Professor Heilprin.

Now, seated in Red Cliff House, Peary was jubilant in his belief that, by reaching the northeast corner, he had proved Greenland to be a giant island. (Later explorations were to show that he had not actually reached the northeastern limits of Greenland. Greenland was found to be an island, but its coast was yet another 100 miles north of Navy Cliff. The westward arm of Independence Bay had tricked him; it did not open into the Arctic Ocean but ran inland. The mountains across the bay, then, were not islands but a part of the northernmost mainland. In later years, some scholars criticized Peary for his error. Others defended him, saying that the mistake was an easy one to make. They added that the error could not really diminish the magnificence of having crossed the Greenland icecap in such northerly latitudes.)

Peary had another reason to be jubilant as he sat there in Red Cliff

House. He knew that his accomplishment would win him the fame that he had sought for so long. In itself, that fame would satisfy a deep hunger in him.

But it would do something even better. It would end the problem of securing funds for his Arctic work. With money now easy to raise, it was certain that he'd be back in the north again soon. And he intended to come back just as soon as possible. In his mind, looming larger than ever before, was that greatest of his goals—the conquest of the North Pole.

Matt looked at Peary and knew what was in the man's mind. And he knew what was in his own mind.

He was now as fascinated as Peary with the Arctic. He didn't know if the explorer planned to bring him along the next time. But that didn't matter. Matt Henson was determined to be with him.

5. Greenland
1893-1895

Peary in Trouble

BECAUSE of the time needed to dismantle the winter quarters, the *Kite* did not sail for home until August 24. Peary, Jo, and Matt used the intervening days to sail one of the whaleboats around Inglefield Gulf, a trip of about 200 miles. The explorer looked on the journey as a relaxing "school-boy's picnic" after the rigors of the icecap and was delighted by all that he saw, especially a small inlet that cut into the Gulf's northern shore like a thin, curving finger. After camping there overnight, he named it Bowdoin Bay in honor of his college. Then he told Matt that it would be an excellent spot for their headquarters when the two of them came north again.

Matt was delighted to know that he'd be with the next expedition. But, on returning to Red Cliff, he began to worry about Peary. Specifically, he began to wonder if the Lieutenant might be a hard-luck explorer, one whose work would always be dogged by misfortune. First, there had been his broken leg. Then those storms that had kept his people from getting his supplies to the icecap ahead of time. Now, with just a few days left before the departure for home, John Verhoeff turned up missing.

The trouble started when Verhoeff and Langdon Gibson asked for permission to take a whaleboat a few miles along McCormick Bay and land at a valley on the northern shore. Gibson wanted to hunt up some more birds for his ornithological collection, and Verhoeff hoped to find some new mineral specimens. Peary saw no reason why they shouldn't go. The *Kite* was still a week away from being loaded and ready for sea.

The men were instructed to return in a few days. Gibson did as he was told and came back on time. But he was alone. He reported that, while they had been scouting the shore, Verhoeff had decided to hike across the valley to Robertson Bay, an inlet located a short distance to the north of McCormick Bay. He'd long wanted to explore there and had asked that the whaleboat be sent to pick him up in three days.

It was an action typical of Verhoeff—a highly independent type of man —and so it didn't surprise Peary. But alarm soon followed. The whaleboat sailed out to collect the mineralogist and returned with the word that he wasn't to be found. Instantly, Peary forgot all else and divided his expedition into search parties.

There was no rest for anyone during the next six days and nights. Peary sent the *Kite* to search the entrance to Robertson Bay. With Matt and a troop of Eskimos, he himself went to the valley where the hike had started and crossed it, after which he scouted all along the Robertson shore. The hunt ended soon after he and Matt came upon a set of bootprints leading up a glacier at the eastern end of the bay.

The two men started to follow the prints up the icy slopes—only to have them disappear after a short distance. Beyond the point of their disappearance, the glacier was cut with a network of deep crevasses.

Matt and Peary exchanged glances. As the explorer later wrote, only one conclusion seemed possible:

"Verhoeff, crossing the glacier, in thick weather perhaps, had slipped and fallen into one of the innumerable yawning crevasses. The accident was the same as those which occur almost annually in the glaciers of the Alps. The great ice-stream where he met his untimely end now bears the name of Verhoeff."

Still, Peary could not bring himself to give up all hope. He and his men carefully searched the entire base of the glacier for some sign that the mineralogist had come back down off the ice. Then, knowing that he could do no more, Peary left a cache of supplies at Robertson Bay. Should Verhoeff still be alive, he'd have food for a year.

Finally, Peary told the Eskimos that they were to go on looking for the young man. If they found him and took good care of him, Peary vowed to "reward them beyond their wildest dreams" when, as he planned, he returned next year.

Feeling as if a gray pall had spread itself over all of the Greenland accomplishments, the searchers returned to Red Cliff. In the next days, the last supplies—including the lumber from the winter house—were stowed aboard the *Kite*. Matt hugged Ikwa and all the other Eskimos in farewell. The *Kite* raised sail on a sunny morning and sailed home— home to fame for Peary, and home to a welter of preparations for the next Arctic adventure.

2.

Matt grinned when the expedition arrived in the United States in September, 1892, and he saw what the newspapers were saying. Sixteen months ago, they had been full of predictions of doom for the Peary expedition. Now they were hailing the explorer and his people as great heroes, and the trip to the northeast corner as a magnificent service to geography. What changes success can bring!

Peary on his return to The United States after the successful crossing of the Greenland icecap in 1892.

He saw the pride that Peary felt and couldn't blame the man for it. The explorer deserved the fame that he had so long sought and that was now coming his way. And it was a fame not just limited to the United States. Word of the icecap journey had been flashed to all parts of the world. Press clippings and letters of praise came flooding in from overseas. Among the latter was a note offering Peary "my most heartfelt congratulations" for "your wonderful achievements and grand results." It was signed by the young Norwegian who had beaten him to the punch on the southern crossing—Fridtjof Nansen.

It was good to receive the congratulations of such a highly respected explorer, but the very name of Nansen filled Matt with worry. The Norwegian still loomed as a dangerous competitor. He'd already beaten Peary once and could well beat him again, this time to that greatest prize of all—the North Pole. The newspapers that were now lauding Peary were also carrying a story about Nansen. They were reporting that he was in the midst of plans for an attack on the Pole.

It was to be an unusual attack. Nansen believed that a major current cut through the Arctic Ocean, shifting the ice pack along a certain line and perhaps carrying it to and across the Pole. He planned to sail a specially built ship—one that wouldn't be crushed by the ice—into the pack at a point where he felt the current ran. Then, locked in the pack, he would float with the current. Hopefully, right to the Pole.

Peary saw the news reports and knew that many scientists felt the scheme to be pretty farfetched, with Nansen having little hope of ever reaching the Pole just by sitting on the ice and going wherever it went. But Peary also knew that he must take no chances with the Norwegian. He must not be cheated of his life's ambition. All during the trip home, he had thought about his plan to return to the northeast corner and see if the islands above Independence Bay could be used as stepping-stones to the Pole. Now he took not a moment to relax. He threw himself into the job of turning the plan into a reality.

Immediately—with Matt watching and trying not to think "hard-luck explorer"—Peary ran into trouble. He asked for a new leave, but the Navy objected, saying that he had already been away from his duties far too long. Further, it was obvious that some of his superiors were envious of his success; as a junior officer, he'd become "too big" to suit them. Only after some influential friends appealed to the Secretary of the Navy and to President Grover Cleveland was the leave finally granted. It was for three years.

Then came another problem. As Peary had expected, a number of scientific organizations were now willing to finance him. But, to his disappointment, their contributions fell far below what he needed and were painfully slow in coming in. By December, he knew that he couldn't depend on the organizations alone. He'd have to do something himself.

He wasn't long in deciding what that "something" would be. The newspapers had fired the public's interest in him and the Arctic. People would be willing to pay good money to see him on a stage and hear him talk about the Greenland adventure. All right. For the first three months of 1893, he'd go on a lecture tour of the Midwest and East, visiting as many cities as he could.

As aloof as he was, he didn't like the idea of standing up on a stage with everyone gawking at him. But if that's what he had to do for his work, then he'd do it. And he'd do something else. He'd give the people a real show, one that would pack the audiences in. He looked at Matt and at the sledges, furs, and six Eskimo dogs that had been brought back from Greenland. They'd all play a part.

The lecture tour proved to be one of the most amusing but uncomfortable experiences of Matt's life—as uncomfortable, he thought wryly at times, as the worst moments in Greenland.

To begin, whenever Peary arrived in a new city, it became Matt's job to publicize that night's talk by putting on his Arctic furs, harnessing the six dogs to a sledge, and taking a two-hour trip through the streets. It was fun to watch shoppers gaping at him from the sidewalks, but, despite the raw winter weather, he found himself sweltering inside the furs. He sweltered even more when the dogs, still as savage as they were back in the Arctic, would sight a stray cat, or a fashionable poodle on a leash. Every ounce of his strength was required to keep the team from dashing after this very delicious-looking prey.

The sledge runs sold many an extra ticket at the box office. But Matt's work didn't end with them. When each lecture began, he was back in his furs, standing offstage with the sledge and perspiring as he kept the team in check. Peary, seeming taller and more heroic than ever in his own furs, walked onto a stage that was made to look like an Eskimo village. After being greeted with warm applause, he called for the lights to be lowered and delivered his talk to the accompaniment of slide pictures of Red Cliff House, McCormick Bay, the icecap, and Navy Cliff. Then, to top everything off, he'd raise his hand in a signal to Matt . . .

Up the stage lights would go to their full brilliance and into their hot glare would come Matt and his team. Shouting "Huk! Huk!"—but hardly able to hear himself above the delighted shrieks of the audience and the clatter of the sledge—he'd circle the stage again and again, at last drawing to a stop alongside Peary. Now it was time for a moment that always made Matt hold his breath.

Peary, explaining that these six dogs had crossed the icecap with him, would invite the audience up for a closer look at them. The bravest of the spectators would venture onstage. And the bravest of their number—with Matt smiling through clenched teeth and daring not the slightest breath now—would lean forward to pat the animals on the head.

Matt had trained the dogs to sit quietly through the ordeal. But he never failed to remember what a battle it had been to get them and their savage brothers into harness back in Greenland. To keep from being bitten, you had to throw yourself at each one from behind and then hold the struggling head and snapping jaws buried in the snow while you slipped the traces into place. Two men were needed to subdue the wildest of the animals. They'd lasso the dog from either side and pull the ropes so tight about his neck that he'd lose consciousness for a moment. In that moment, they'd spring forward with the traces. It had all seemed very cruel—and was—but it had been the only way of getting the job done.

Fortunately, the six dogs always behaved themselves and the spectators escaped without a nip. While Matt started to breathe again, Peary would have a few more things to say. Within several minutes, the dogs themselves would usually put an end to the evening. Becoming bored with it all, they'd sit back on their haunches and begin to howl, continuing until Peary bade his happy audience good night and Matt guided the sledge offstage.

The tour—which saw 168 lectures delivered in 103 days—left Peary and Matt exhausted. But the profits more than made up for the tiredness. The talks brought in a total of $20,000. After deducting expenses, Peary had $13,000 for his expedition. With the money received from the scientific organizations, it put him over the top.

Once the financial problem was out of the way, the final details for the journey north came together. For a time, Matt thought that he was reliving the 1891 preparations. The last supplies were bought. A ship was chartered—not the *Kite* this time but a black-hulled barkentine called the *Falcon*. Her captain was Harry Bartlett and he sailed her from her home base at Newfoundland to Philadelphia, where everything from sledges to timber for the winter house was stowed aboard. Long before the ship arrived, Peary was interviewing men who wanted to go to Greenland as helpers.

In all, the explorer decided on eleven companions. Matt and Eivand Astrup were automatic selections, as was Dr. Cook. The doctor, however, withdrew at the last moment, leaving Matt and Astrup as the only veterans of the 1891-92 trip. The new members were: Dr. Edwin E. Vincent, who would be the expedition's physician; Evelyn Briggs Baldwin, meteorologist; Frederick Stokes, an artist; and Samuel J. Entrikin, George F. Clark, James Davidson, George H. Carr, Walter F. Swain, and a young and smallish newspaperman named Hugh J. Lee, all of whom were listed as assistants.

The lecture tour had taken Matt's mind off his worries about Peary. Now, when he saw how large the expedition was to be, they came flooding back. In signing on so many men, the explorer was flying right in the face of his basic belief that a small party always had the best chances for success. But, on hearing Matt voice his concern, Peary had a ready answer.

He said that at least eight men would be needed for the journey to the northeast corner. Why? Because, on arriving at Independence Bay, he planned to divide them into three groups. The first group would probe northward to see how far the islands above the Bay extended into the

*The young newspaper-
man Hugh J. Lee proved
to be one of Peary's
most loyal and coura-
geous men.*

Arctic Ocean. The second group would travel in the opposite direction—
southward along the east coast to Cape Bismarck. No one had ever
visited that section of coast before and the group was to map it. The third
group would remain at Independence Bay, hunt for musk oxen, and store
up a supply of fresh meat for use when the expedition reassembled and
started back to home base.

Peary now leaned forward and said that he had something to tell Matt
in confidence.

He started by saying that he'd always talked about going to the North
Pole in the future. But now, with Nansen planning a Pole trip, he knew
that he couldn't wait for the future. He was keeping it all secret because
he didn't want the Norwegian to hurry his own expedition, but he was

going to travel north from Independence Bay with the first of the three groups. If the islands carried him far enough into the Arctic Ocean, he then planned to push right on the rest of the way to the Pole!

Matt nodded. He assured Peary that the secret was safe with him. It was an exciting secret and the excitement showed in Matt's dark face. But, inside, he felt himself being torn in two directions.

On the one hand, there was the thirsting hope that he'd be one of the eight chosen to go with Peary to the northeast corner and then—he almost dared not to think of this—on toward the Pole itself. He must not be made to relive the disappointment of 1892 when he'd been left behind. He wanted desperately to be recognized as an explorer and not just as a servant.

But, on the other hand, Matt felt a deep sense of unease. The expedition seemed far too ambitious and involved too many men, most of them greenhorns to the rigors of the Arctic. Too many things could go wrong. It was all too dangerous for a man who might be a hard-luck explorer.

3.

Matt's uneasiness persisted throughout the final weeks of preparation and was clinging to him when the *Falcon* raised anchor at Philadelphia on June 26, 1893, sailed down the Delaware River, and swung into the Atlantic. The expedition seemed off to a miserable start. The weather was bad, rainy and cold. And the news had just come in that, quite by coincidence, Nansen was setting out from Norway on this very day. Everyone on board hoped that he would be long months in finding his suspected current and then floating with it to the top of the world.

Far more worrisome in Matt's opinion, however, was the fact that Jo was aboard with a woman companion, the formidable Mrs. Susan J. Cross. Under ordinary circumstances, after all that Jo had done on the first expedition, Matt would have welcomed her presence. But her circumstances were anything but ordinary for a woman heading into the

*Matt at the time of the
1893–95 expedition to
Greenland.*

Arctic. She was pregnant. The baby was due in September, about a month after the scheduled arrival in Greenland.

Once again, Jo had said flatly that she wouldn't be separated from her husband. And, once again, Peary hadn't argued, insisting only that Mrs. Cross come along as nurse and midwife. He clearly felt that if Eskimo babies could be safely born in the Arctic, so could his child. The newspapers and the couple's friends had said that they had both taken leave of their senses. The troubled but closed-mouth Matt agreed.

But he felt all his worries begin to fade when the *Falcon* knifed into Baffin Bay after brief stops at Maine, Newfoundland, and Labrador. There, as before, were the tumbled shores of Greenland, with the icecap glittering high behind them. And there, as before, were the majestic fleets of icebergs floating silently by on all sides. But not there this year was the heavy ice pack that had made life so hard for the *Kite*. There was some pack, of course, but it split apart easily and the *Falcon* seemed to fly past Cape York. Perhaps everything was going to be all right, after all.

Peary's destination was Bowdoin Bay, the finger-shaped inlet where he had camped with Jo and Matt during last year's tour of Inglefield Gulf. Now, marking a fitting end to an easy voyage, Matt saw that the entrance to the Gulf was free of ice. Doing what the *Kite* had been unable to do, the *Falcon* turned into that broad expanse of water, angled over to the northern shore, and entered Bowdoin Bay.

The expedition went ashore at the head of the Bay, in an area sheltered by rising slopes. Delighted, Peary and Jo found a dozen rocks set in a circle safely up from the water's edge; still in place after all these months, they had been used to hold down the skirts of the Peary tent during last year's visit. He ordered the winter house—which he then christened Anniversary Lodge in memory of the visit—to be built about fifty feet away.

With everyone working round-the-clock, the house was completed by August 20. By that date also, all supplies were ashore. The *Falcon*, with letters aboard for friends and loved ones in the United States, departed for home. She'd be back, Captain Harry Bartlett promised, not in one year this time but two. The extra months would be needed for the work that the expedition would do when it was split into three groups upon reaching Independence Bay.

When the *Falcon* had first entered the Gulf, she had been sighted, and soon the Eskimo workers of last year were sledging in to balloon the ranks of the expedition. There were bursts of laughter, bear hugs, and shouts of "Miy Paluk" when Ikwa and Ahnalka sighted Matt; right away, they made him prove that he hadn't forgotten how to speak Eskimo and drive a sledge. Then, on September 12, the expedition grew by yet another member—a nine-pound baby daughter for the Pearys.

The proud parents said that she was the first white child to be born this far in the north. They called her Marie and gave her the strange middle name of Ahnighito—strange, that is, unless you were a Greenlander and knew that it belonged to the Eskimo woman who had patiently chewed the bird skins that were to serve as the child's first clothing.

The Eskimos soon gave the new arrival a name of their own. To them, because of her white skin and fair hair, she was the "Snow Baby." Peary later wrote that the infant "was the source of liveliest interest to the natives. Entire families journeyed from faraway Cape York to the south, and from distant Etah to the north, to satisfy themselves by actual touch that she was a creature of warm flesh and blood, and not of snow, as they first believed."

The safe birth of little Marie was a happy event. But it turned out to be the last happy event for the expedition. For the second time since the lecture tour, all of Matt's old misgivings came rushing back as, in the next months, everything went wrong.

First, there was the sad truth to be faced about the missing Verhoeff. Ever since the *Falcon* had neared Cape York, Peary had scanned the coastline for some glimpse of the man and had stopped at the Cape itself for a brief search. Now, as the Eskimos arrived in camp, he asked if they had anything to report. At first, they were hesitant to answer. Then, admitting that they were always fearful of speaking of the dead, they said that they had seen nothing of the mineralogist throughout the long winter.

Peary listened with a grim face. All the hope that had remained in him—and there hadn't been much—faded away. There could be no doubt left that Verhoeff was entombed, never to be found, somewhere up on the glacier that now bore his name.

No sooner had the truth about Verhoeff been accepted than there was trouble with Astrup. As in 1891, Peary wanted supplies cached up on

Marie Ahnighito Peary, born at Anniversary Lodge on September 12, 1893. Because of her fair skin, the Eskimos called her the "Snow Baby."

the icecap before winter fell. But now, because he was going to make the crossing with so many men, he wanted the supplies spread out over the first 100 miles of the coming journey. He gave Astrup the job of putting them in place and assigned James Davidson, George Carr, and diminutive Hugh Lee to him as helpers. The party started for the icecap with five Eskimo-driven sledges on August 29. They were back on September 13—with bad news and with Astrup suffering stomach cramps.

Edwin Vincent, the expedition's doctor, examined Astrup and diagnosed the problem as gastric fever. Astrup was sent to bed and his services were lost to the expedition for several weeks. As for the supply caches, the bad news there was that the party had managed to sledge a mere twelve miles out on the icecap before a storm had pinned them

The Falcon *at anchor below Anniversary Lodge.*

down. They had stored the supplies there, had marked them with flags, and turned for home with Astrup.

Peary sent the three helpers back to the cap with fresh loads. Two days later, he and Matt sledged out to join them with additional loads. It was the first of a number of trips that Peary, accompanied at one time or another by practically everyone of his men, made in the next weeks. They were trips that continued through October and into early November, long after the Arctic night had closed down. All of them were marked with trouble. One storm after another hit the Americans.

Once, the wind lifted three emptied sledges and blew them away; hours were lost in locating them. On another day, it knocked Carr to the ice; his back was so badly wrenched that, like Astrup, he was bedridden for

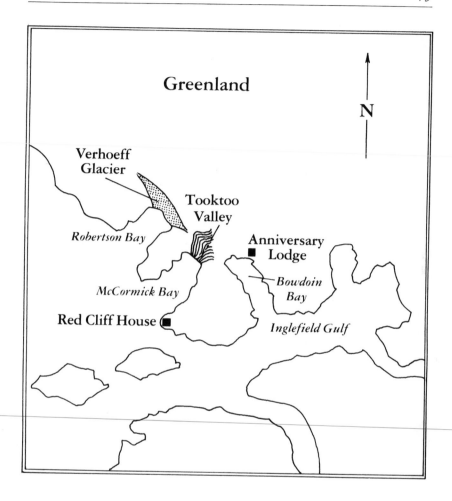

weeks. One man froze two fingers and a thumb. By mid-November, when Peary called it quits for the winter, the supplies were cached just twenty-six miles out on the cap.

Things were hardly any better back at Anniversary Lodge. Peary had brought along eight burros from New Mexico as an experiment to see if they could be of any service in Arctic exploration. A couple were attacked by the Eskimo dogs, whose instincts told them that these strange creatures would make a tasty meal. The others sickened and died with the cold before doing any real work.

The same fate befell the carrier pigeons that the explorer hoped to use for exchanging messages between his icecap party and Anniversary Lodge. Only one managed to get through with a message during the supply cache trips. Others flew off with messages and were never seen again. Others died of the cold. And one made the fatal mistake of sticking his head out of his cage while a hungry dog was sitting and waiting just inches away.

Then, topping everything off, one morning a wall of ice broke away from a nearby glacier and plunged into the sea. It created a giant wave that, tossing aside the floes that lay in its path, rolled up Bowdoin Bay and slammed into the winter camp.

Anniversary Lodge itself, built on high ground, was not hit. But there was devastation everywhere else. The wave caught a whaleboat and swept her along, spinning this way and that, for a hundred yards; her sides were shattered by the boulders that got in the way. A steam launch went bottom-up and was stove in. When the wave receded, it carried away a dory and all the barrels of oil that Peary had brought north for heating the camp. No one ever saw the dory again, but fortunately most of the barrels, dented and twisted out of shape, were cast up along the Bay shores and retrieved.

When it was all over, Matt surveyed the damage and shook his head. The expedition was turning into a disaster. How much worse, he wondered, could things get?

He was to find out in the spring. It was then that the very worst came.

6. Greenland
1893-1895

Hard-luck Expedition

FOR Matt, the worst came when, just before spring dawned, he learned that he wasn't going to be picked for the eight-man icecap party. Once again, Peary wanted him to remain with Jo. He was to see that no harm befell her during the explorer's absence and then was to help her get the baby and Mrs. Cross safely home if the crossing ended in death.

Matt felt a knifelike disappointment. And—even though Peary was paying him the compliment of entrusting three lives to his care—a sudden and hard anger. Peary's trust was just one part of the story. There were others in camp who could help Jo just as much as he. There was, he knew, another reason for leaving him behind.

That reason? Matt's good sense told him that it had nothing to do with his color. Peary wasn't prejudiced; nor did the explorer, though aloof by nature, look down on him as an inferior human being. If either had ever been the case, Peary would never have brought him north to begin with, not even as a servant. The reason, instead, had to do with one of the explorer's many ideas on how best to run an expedition.

Long ago, Peary had decided that wiry, intelligent, and well-educated men had the best chances of surviving in the wilds and completing their assignments. They had the stamina (far more, Peary believed, than the biggest muscle men), the brains, and the training to meet any emergency or hardship. Starting in Nicaragua, the lithe Matt had proven his stamina and intelligence. But he lacked an extensive formal education. He may have read his way through Captain Childs' library, but he was the only man at Bowdoin Bay without a college education.

And so there was no escaping one fact. Because he could not measure up to one of Peary's high standards, he was to be left behind and an Arctic greenhorn was to go up on the icecap in his place.

He wanted to shout out that the explorer was making a terrible mistake. Peary's faith in education had blinded him to the value of practical experience. He was leaving behind his best igloo builder, his best sledge driver. And the one man besides Astrup who knew how to build and repair sledges.

Ever since arriving at Bowdoin Bay, Matt had been building extra sledges as backups for the ones that Peary had brought north. Some had been used on the supply runs; some would make the crossing. Matt was proud of them. Into them all he'd put fine American spruce and the best of his carpentry skills. Now, with their builder left behind, what would Peary do when, as was sure to happen, some accident befell them? And if Astrup, perhaps injured or sick again, was in no condition to fix them?

But Matt did not shout out. He knew that it would do no good, that Peary would always run his expeditions as he himself saw fit. All that he could do was to go on working loyally and hoping that one day the man would recognize his true worth.

And so, choking back his anger and disappointment, he helped to load the icecap sledges with the food crates, rifles, ammunition, and deerskin sleeping bags that would be needed in addition to the supplies already cached. Then, on March 6, 1894, he stood with Jo and watched Peary begin the run northeast.

Compared with the 1892 start from Red Cliff, this one seemed almost awesome. With Peary were seven white men, five Eskimos, twelve sledges, and ninety-two dogs. The party looked like a small army, warmly clad and well equipped for any battle that might come. But when Matt saw his "brothers," the five Eskimos, his heart sank a little. All that he could find etched in their leathery faces was fear.

He understood their fear. They dreaded the icecap and, like all Greenland Eskimos, never went near it. A motionless thunder cloud that dominated their horizon, it was the home of the great devil, Kokoyah. He protected his icy domain with bottomless crevasses that swallowed intruders, razor-edge *sastrugi* (ice ridges formed by the wind) that tore their boots to ribbons, and wild storms that froze them to death if they didn't have the sense to run away. Only after the promise of such riches as cooking utensils and rifles did five of the bravest Eskimos in camp agree to help Peary sledge a few miles out onto the cap. Then they were to turn for home.

Though he didn't take their superstitious beliefs seriously, Matt winced at their fear. It reminded him of just how afraid he himself was for Peary. Would all the bad luck of the past months follow the explorer up into the mists and prove to be his own Kokoyah? For Matt, the worst had already come. He had the cold, sick feeling that, for Peary, the worst was now to come.

2.

He was right. The expedition was doomed to failure from the moment that Peary sledged onto the icecap.

The trouble started on March 10. Suddenly, a dog that had been perfectly well just minutes before was frothing at the mouth, and the Eskimos were shouting in alarm. The animal threw himself wildly from side to side in his traces, snapped at his teammates, and finally got his teeth into the neck of one. A veteran now of two winters in the Arctic, Peary knew what he was seeing. This was the hated disease that the Eskimos called *piblockto*.

Though no one understood its cause, it seemed to be a form of hydrophobia and was perhaps triggered by long exposure to the intense cold. To the Eskimos, it was a frightening madness that always ended in a horrible death. The animals died in agony, blindly attacking anything in sight and threatening to sicken all the other animals with their bites because the disease was contagious. There was only one way to end the victim's misery and protect the teams. Peary raised his rifle and took careful aim.

Two days later, there was more trouble, but of a different sort. At the end of a long uphill climb, Peary saw that Hugh Lee was limping. Last month, Lee had frozen a toe while on a sledge run to check on how the icecap supply caches had survived the winter. Now Peary and Dr. Vincent saw that he had frozen it anew. Over some pretty stiff objections, Peary told the young newspaperman that he couldn't go on without danger of losing the toe. He'd have to return to Anniversary Lodge.

Then Peary looked up to find Eivand Astrup at his shoulder. Astrup's face was pale and tight with pain. He said that his stomach cramps of last year had returned. Peary nodded. Astrup must go back with Lee.

Their loss filled Peary with a deep sense of foreboding. He'd been on the trail for just six days and already he was down by two men. If the same thing went on happening, he wouldn't have enough men left to split the expedition into the planned three groups when he reached Independence Bay. If, indeed, he reached the Bay at all. In these past six days, he'd traveled a scant thirty-five miles.

As expected, the five Eskimos turned for home in another day or two, having come as far into Kokoyah's dreaded territory as they dared. Peary sledged on eastward until March 22 when a storm came hurtling down the icecap. A howling wind swept the snowdrift up from the ice and drove it, needle-sharp, into the men's faces. The temperature plunged to 35° below zero. Peary called the sledges to a halt. Leaving the dogs where they were in their traces, he ordered that two tents be erected. The dogs burrowed into the snow, curled themselves into balls with their noses beneath their tails, and prepared to sleep the storm away.

The tents held three men each. Peary, Samuel Entrikin, and George Clark crawled into one. Living on tea and pea soup heated over an alcohol burner, they lay huddled together for a day and a night. Then they were joined by their companions from the other tent. The newcomers said that their tent flap had been unable to hold the flying snowdrift at bay. The stuff had come swirling in so hard that it had threatened to bury them.

Outside, the storm raged for another day, sending the temperature down another five degrees. Nevertheless, Peary later wrote, he and his friends had remained "warm and comfortable" in their animal-skin clothing. But they couldn't have been otherwise comfortable. Crowded beyond its capacity, the tent had space for just five men to sit or lie down at a time. The sixth had to stand, supporting himself by holding onto the center pole. The men took turns standing.

When the storm finally ended, Peary went outside and looked "upon a scene that made me sick at heart. Half my dogs were frozen fast in the snow, some by the legs, and all were in pitiable condition, their fur a mass of ice and snow driven into it by the pitiless wind. Several of the animals had chewed their way out of their traces. In a wild search for food, they'd attacked the sledges and destroyed several sleeping bags. They'd also found some extra harnesses and had gnawed the leather to shreds."

As battered as the dogs were, they were ready for the trail as soon as they had downed a good meal. But this wasn't true of James Davidson. In making the transfer to Peary's tent during the storm, he had frozen a heel and could hardly walk. Peary ordered him back to Anniversary Lodge, then told Dr. Vincent to go along also because there would now be three men back there in need of medical care. Left on the icecap with Peary were Samuel Entrikin, George Clark, and meteorologist Evelyn Briggs Baldwin.

It was a discouraged Peary who pushed on northeast. Gone now were all thoughts of splitting the expedition into three groups. The great plan was dead. He had just enough men left to try a probe of the islands north of Independence Bay and perhaps a run toward the Pole. But he shook his head. Would the men have the strength to travel farther once they'd reached Navy Cliff? Would *he*?

In the end, these were questions that he never had to answer. The icecap—or perhaps it was Kokoyah—seemed determined to keep him from reaching the northeast corner and it finally won out. Entrikin froze the bottoms of both feet. Then, as he was fighting to get his sledge across some especially high *sastrugi*, he strained his back. Clark's breath, condensing in the frigid air, froze his furs so hard one day that, as Peary later wrote, "he could neither walk nor turn his head . . ." On another day, Clark awoke to find that his nose had frozen itself to the facial opening in his sleeping bag. Peary, as on the 1892 crossing, began to suffer from snow blindness.

Then a new storm boiled in. It lasted for forty-eight hours, buried all the dogs in snow, and froze two of them to death. Finally, topping everything off, three dogs were struck with *piblockto*. Before they could be shot, they rampaged through the teams and attacked practically every one of their remaining fellows.

Since the 1892 crossing had taken about a month each way, Peary had planned to arrive at Independence Bay sometime during the first week of April. On April 10, he took stock of his situation and admitted a terrible truth: he was beaten. In all this time, he'd struggled for just a quarter of the distance across the cap and was a mere 128 miles from Anniversary Lodge. His men were all in bad shape. His dog teams were seriously depleted, and the *sastrugi* had battered his sledges to pieces. He himself was exhausted and half blind. It was impossible to go on.

But, even as he told the men that he was turning back, he knew that he was not admitting *total* defeat. He'd been stopped this time, but he was going to return again, hopefully next spring; the *Falcon* had still more than another full year before it was due back at Anniversary Lodge. Even in this most sickening of moments, the ambition to reach the Pole still burned hot. To help with the next attempt, Peary unloaded most of his remaining supplies—over 1,000 pounds' worth—and cached them on the ice. He marked the spot with a nine-foot pole, bracing it firmly. He was sure that it could be seen from a distance of two or three miles.

Then he and his three men turned their haggard, wind-bitten faces westward. En route, they left behind two small caches—one about fifty miles out from Bowdoin Bay, the other about twenty-six miles distant. On April 20, they were back in the warmth of Anniversary Lodge.

3.

In the next days, Matt and Jo had an exhausted man on their hands. Peary slept almost continuously, rousing himself only now and again to take some hot food or to be checked by Dr. Vincent. Out in the main room of the Lodge, his three companions slept just as soundly.

At last, there was enough sleep. But now, in the aftermath of defeat, there came a deep depression. Matt heard the explorer tell Jo again and again that he'd been a fool: he'd forgotten his fundamental belief that small parties have the best chance of survival in the Arctic. He'd taken along too many men. He'd been too ambitious and the cap had made him pay for the mistake. He wanted to cross again next spring. But who of his men would again follow him after he had made such a mess of things? Yet he dared not go home without another try. The newspapers would brand him a failure. He couldn't stand that.

A worried Matt had never seen his employer so discouraged. But, as

Peary's full strength returned in the next weeks, the black mood faded and the busy mind turned again to exploring. Peary wanted to do something to keep this year from being a complete waste. But what? Then he remembered an Arctic story he had read as a boy . . .

The story came from the great British explorer, Captain John Ross. In 1818, while anchored at Cape York, he'd met several Eskimos carrying iron knives, a startling sight in this barren and primitive land. They explained that they had cut the weapons from some "mountains" to the south, in the Melville Bay area. But, obviously afraid that the white man would steal their treasured metal, they refused to show Ross where the mountains were and fell silent to all further questions.

Only a few Eskimos seemed to know the location of the "iron mountains" and they were just as silent with all the other explorers who ventured north in the next decades. In 1892, however, Peary had managed to pry a little information out of a few Eskimo workers at Red Cliff. From what they said, he was pretty sure that the mountains weren't mountains at all but meteorites instead. Long, long ago—so local legend held—the irons had been thrown down from the sky by an angry Tornarsuk, the greatest of all the far northern devils. In all, there were three irons.

Peary had wanted to go looking for them then, but there hadn't been the time. Now, he decided, he'd come to the perfect moment for a search; not only would their discovery salvage the year but it would be an accomplishment that would save him from being branded a failure. He knew that several of the Eskimos in camp had visited the irons at one time or another. He approached them and offered a rifle as payment for being guided to the spot. One young man wasted no time in reaching for the rifle.

Peary and a sledge pulled by ten dogs left for Melville Bay on May 16. With him went the young newspaperman, Hugh Lee, now pretty well recovered from his frozen toe. They were gone for three weeks. When they returned, they brought a story of success.

With their guide, they had first sledged over to Cape York. Then, joined by an aging Eskimo named Tallakoteah, they had headed for Melville Bay. En route, Peary learned that Tallakoteah had some very precise information about the irons. Confirmed was his suspicion that they were meteorites. One, the oldster said, was a stone about the size of a dog and had been given that name by the Eskimos. Another was somewhat larger and resembled a woman in a sitting position. She had broad shoulders and, on top of them, there had once been an outcrop that looked like a head. Years ago, someone had broken the head off and carted it away.

When Tornarsuk had thrown them down from the sky, Tallakoteah went on, the "woman" and the "dog" had landed just a few yards from each other on a strip of Melville Bay coast. But the third had come down on a small island just offshore. It was the largest of the trio. The Eskimos called it the "tent."

On reaching Melville Bay, Tallakoteah led the Americans to a stretch of rocky coast. Grinning, he stopped and said that they had reached their destination. Peary looked about and—startled—saw nothing but desolate beach.

But Tallakoteah didn't seem in the least worried. He began digging in a patch of snow nearby. Peary and Lee joined him. Soon, they had dug out a hole five feet in diameter and three feet deep. And there, showing her brown shoulders, was the "woman." The two Americans were the first white men ever to see her. Fascinated, they watched as Tallakoteah demonstrated how the Eskimos cut into the iron and then shaped the takings into knives.

The Eskimo then pointed to where he thought the "dog" lay beneath the snow. But the small meteorite was down too deep for their shovels. Peary had to content himself with marking the shore with a rock cairn and carving the initial P in the woman to prove his discovery. Likewise, he had to content himself with a brief visit to the island where the "tent" was located. It, too, was buried beyond reach.

The work done, Peary turned north toward Anniversary Lodge. He told Lee that he planned to return to the site of the irons one day soon. He wanted to transport them home for the world to see. His hope was to sell them to a museum and then use the money to help finance his future Arctic work. It was an idea that later earned him much criticism. Many people thought it unfair of him to remove a treasure so much needed by the inhabitants of this barren land.

Back at Anniversary Lodge, life had been passing quietly for Matt. He helped Jo with the household chores and hunted for game with his Eskimo friends. Often, he took little Marie for sled rides along the shores of Bowdoin Bay. Squealing with delight, she was bundled in furs and strapped to the upstanders of a tiny sled that her father had built for her and that was pulled by the two gentlest dogs in camp. Riding along with her was her favorite playmate, five-year-old Kudlooktoo.

Kudlooktoo was the son of one of the women who had spent the winter at Red Cliff sewing furs for the 1892 crossing. She had died some months ago and, ever since, the child had lived with various Eskimo families because his hunter father was rarely at home. On first seeing him at Anniversary Lodge, Matt had immediately taken a liking to this sturdy little boy with the buttonlike brown eyes. He'd bathed the youngster, trimmed his hair, and dressed him in clean clothes. Kudlooktoo now slept at the foot of Matt's bed and was known as his "adopted son." They would meet again and again in the Arctic as the years passed.

When Peary returned to Anniversary Lodge, it seemed to Matt that the two children were about the only happy people in camp. Matt knew that most of the explorer's men were bitterly disappointed with the failure up on the icecap. Further, they were still suffering the effects of frozen hands, feet, and faces, and were terribly homesick. All these things made them forget that they had volunteered to come north with Peary. They now blamed him for bringing them here and exposing them to such hardships. And they did nothing to hide their feelings from him.

Their behavior caused Matt to grit his teeth. Even in his own anguish at being passed over for the crossing, he had never acted as they did now. Several questioned Peary's abilities as a leader. Dr. Vincent was openly rude to him on occasion.

Matt looked at a calendar and shook his head. The *Falcon* was not due to return for another year. How in heaven's name would Peary and the men survive together for that length of time in the close confines of Anniversary Lodge?

But he needn't have worried. On July 31, an Eskimo burst into camp. The man shouted excitedly that he'd just seen a ship pushing its way through the ice near Cape York. A short time later, the *Falcon*'s familiar black hull coasted into Bowdoin Bay. Captain Harry Bartlett came ashore with the news that the Pearys' relatives and friends had been so worried about Jo and the new baby that they had financed an early return of the *Falcon*. They had asked Bartlett to bring Jo and Marie home, along with anyone else who needed or wanted to leave.

Both Peary and Jo agreed that it would be wise to take Marie back to civilization. But the explorer had no intention of accompanying them. He was as determined as ever to hike again to the northeast corner when the spring of 1895 arrived. And—because Bartlett had brought word that the Nansen expedition was still floating around on the Arctic Ocean ice and had not yet reached the North Pole—he was more determined than ever to push on to the islands above Independence Bay and see where they led.

He then drew Matt to one side and told him something that had appalled Jo. Since he had no idea of when he'd be back, he didn't want the *Falcon* to return again next summer; he had no wish to have Bartlett sitting here and waiting for him and perhaps getting caught in the ice of the following winter. Instead, at the end of his exploration, he would return to Anniversary Lodge for a short rest. Then he would sledge over to Cape York and travel down the western face of Greenland until he came upon the whalers that visited Baffin Bay annually. He'd "hitch" a ride home aboard one of them.

It was a risky plan, Peary admitted. He was going to ask for volunteers to accompany him, but from the way the men had been acting, he didn't think he'd get many. Whoever went would be out on the ice for months. In the main, they'd have to live off the supplies cached up on the cap and off whatever game they managed to shoot. And, at the end of things, they might have to hike for weeks before sighting a whaler.

Peary looked straight at Matt. It had been a hard-luck expedition so far. But would Matt be willing to take the risk? Would he come along?

Matt felt his heart leap. Of course he'd go. After all the years of being a servant, his life was again changing—and as suddenly as always. At last, he was going to be the one thing that he was willing to take any risk for. He was going to be an explorer.

7. Greenland
1893-1895

Three Against Death

MATT had always liked Hugh Lee. Though the young news-paperman was small in stature and a bit frail-looking, he had long ago shown that he had a tough, strong mind. During the preparations back in Philadelphia, he had written a letter asking to be picked for the expedition and then had gone several weeks without a reply from the busy Peary. At last, no longer able to keep his patience in check, he had fired off a postcard.

In it, he had politely but firmly demanded that the explorer give him an answer. Peary, he said, shouldn't keep him "suspended between heaven and earth" any longer.

Peary had grinned at this display of spirit and, sight unseen, had chosen Lee for the expedition. The choice had been a good one. Lee had worked hard, taking on any job assigned to him. And he hadn't been among those who had complained after everything had ended in failure. In particular, his great sense of pride had won Matt's heart. Matt remembered seeing how Lee and Astrup had come into camp last spring when Peary had sent them back from the crossing. Astrup had been lying on a sledge. But Lee, gritting his teeth with the pain of his frozen toe, had been walking.

And now, a year later, on this Sunday night of March 31, 1895, here was Lee in Anniversary Lodge, the only man to join Matt in staying with Peary for a second attack on the icecap. Matt watched the young man shave and ready himself for tomorrow. Tomorrow—the day when the assault would begin.

Watching, Matt felt a fresh wave of liking for Lee. It came as his mind went back to last August when the *Falcon* had lain at anchor out there in Bowdoin Bay.

He could see Peary again, going from one to the other of his men and asking if they would remain for the winter and then try a new crossing come spring. Each had shaken a head, some in regret, some in anger at the thought of being asked to take such a risk after the hardships already suffered. Matt remembered how each turndown had wounded the explorer's great pride. But then there had been the day when Peary approached Lee.

Matt had been standing in the doorway of the Lodge. He watched the pair walk along the beach and he saw Peary talking earnestly. After a time, the two men stopped and faced each other. Then—miracle of miracles—Lee nodded. Peary actually dropped back a step in surprise and, even at a distance, the smile that broke over his face was plain to see. Peary extended his hand and Lee took it . . .

And so, Matt now thought, it was to be three men against the icecap. The *Falcon* was long gone. Their sledges were loaded and ready to start. Their dogs were in harness. Six Eskimos had agreed to help them on their way by accompanying them for several days. Waiting out on the icecap were the three supply caches that Peary had set down when returning from last year's crossing.

The caches were all waiting—that is, if they hadn't been buried beyond reach in the snow and if the wind hadn't blown their marker poles away.

Yes, everyone was ready to go. But, Matt thought, the trio really seemed too puny to be attacking the vicious Kokoyah's domain. Courageous though Lee was, he was far from physically fit. He'd been plagued with grippe for much of the winter. Matt had also been down with it. And Peary had wrenched his back painfully while doing some work. If Matt let himself think about it, 1895 seemed to promise as much disaster as 1894 . . .

But he wouldn't let himself think about it. He walked across the room to the wall where his animal-skin outfit for the journey was hanging. He told himself that he must think of only one thing: he was twenty-eight years old and tomorrow, wearing these reindeer-skin trousers and his thick jacket with its fur headpiece, he'd be an explorer for the first time.

2.

They started early in the morning, right after a hot breakfast. Pulled by sixty dogs, there were six sledges in the party, divided equally between the Americans and the Eskimos. Matt walked at the upstanders of the largest; it carried tents, bedding, and the food supplies that Peary hoped to save until the return trip. Peary's sledge was also loaded with food—mainly raw, frozen reindeer meat—but it was to be eaten on the outbound journey. Aboard Lee's sledge was 750 pounds of walrus meat for the dogs.

As usual, the uphill climb over the rocks and tumbled brown earth proved to be difficult. But, Matt thought, Peary couldn't have picked a better day for a start. The weather was clear and the air crisp—not a hint of a storm anywhere. If only the weather will hold, Matt told himself. We'll really make some time.

The weather did hold. In two days, the party was on the icecap, and the odometer on Peary's sledge was showing that they had reached the site of the first supply cache. But, as he'd expected, the cache was nowhere in sight. Armed with saw-knives and shovels, the men spread out from the sledges. They investigated every hump in the ice, with Matt helping to dig several five-foot-deep pits and then shaking his head in disappointment over them all. At last, Peary said that the cache was irretrievably buried. No more time should be wasted on it.

Peary walked back to the sledges with Matt. The explorer recalled that the cache contained fourteen cases of biscuit, three cases of condensed milk, and 100 pounds of pea soup. He didn't like to leave these treasures behind, but he said that their loss was not really critical. The truly important cache was the third one—the big one that lay 128 miles out on the ice.

Another day's march brought the party to the site of the second—and smallest—of the caches. Once again, nothing was to be seen. But, in the search that followed, a keen-eyed dog sighted something in the snow. It turned out to be the top three inches of the nine-foot pole that had been left to mark the cache. When dug out, the cache yielded ten cases of biscuit and a case and a half of condensed milk.

The weather continued to behave gently, with no severe winds and with the temperatures warm—warm, that is, by Arctic standards. They hovered between 12° and 14° below zero while, for three days in a row, the sledges literally flew over the ice. At last, Peary raised his hand and signaled for a halt. He walked back to Matt's sledge to say that, according to his compass and odometer, they were at the third and final cache.

Matt shook his head in wonder. They had reached a point 128 miles from Anniversary Lodge. Last year, it had taken a month of indescribable hardship for Peary to come this far. This time, the same distance had been covered in a mere six days. Matt glanced skyward. Somewhere up there, that old devil Kokoyah must be dozing in the good weather . . .

But, if indeed Kokoyah had been dozing, he awakened now and frowned. Things started to go wrong. As before, there was no sign of the cache, and Peary sent the Eskimos sledging into the distance to search for the marker pole. With Matt and Lee, he covered the ice all around the sledges. The hunt lasted for a full and fruitless twenty-four hours. The marker pole was gone, most likely blown away by the vicious winds.

Peary dropped to his sledge and sat looking up at Matt and Lee. His shoulders were slumping for the first time. The cache would never be found, he said, and its loss was a "staggering blow" to the expedition. It was the one setback that he had dreaded above all others.

Both Matt and Lee knew why. Along with the game that could be shot once they came off the far side of the icecap, there was just enough food aboard the sledges to get them to—and perhaps a little beyond—Independence Bay and then back to base camp. Buried somewhere here were more than 1,000 pounds in foodstuffs. Peary had wanted these supplies desperately for safety's sake and for the extra exploring time north of the Bay they would give him.

And, of equal importance, he had wanted them as a health insurance. They were made up chiefly of pemmican, that nourishing concoction whose principal ingredient was beef. Working as hard as they were, the Americans couldn't long survive on frozen reindeer meat. Nor could the dogs live on walrus only. Man and animal alike needed fresh meat. The pemmican would serve well in its place until some game could be bagged. Without it, there would soon be weakness and illness. And, in time, death.

Of course, there was some pemmican aboard the sledges. But it wouldn't last for long.

The explorer looked from man to man. A decision must be made, he said. But, because it involved their lives and not just his, he could not make it alone. Should they continue northeast without the pemmican? Or turn back? If they failed to find any game at Independence Bay, they'd be in desperate straits . . .

Both men checked him in mid-sentence. They hadn't come this far only to quit. They'd stick with him—right to the end.

Matt was sure that he saw strength come pouring back into Peary's face. He heard a quiet "thank you."

But, as Peary started up from the sledge, Matt touched his shoulder. Before they moved on, Matt said, something should be done about the Eskimos. For days now, as the sledges had penetrated ever deeper into Kokoyah's territory, he had seen the Eskimos growing more frightened and more certain that, at any moment, the great devil would punish their intrusion with a killer storm. They had bravely stayed on and had done more than their part. It was time to send them home.

Peary agreed, and the Eskimos greeted the news with relief. Quickly, they transferred the supplies from their sledges to the Peary rigs, leaving themselves just enough food for the homeward marches. Then, after there had been hugs and handshakes all around, they were on their way. Matt watched them until they were no more than brown dots on the endless white surface.

He turned northeast. But lingering in his mind, refusing to go away, was the memory of how the Eskimos had looked when they had come to bid him farewell. There had been a deep sorrow in their eyes—as if they were saying good-bye to their brother for the last time.

3.

With the Eskimos and their sledges gone, Peary was left with forty-two dogs. In the next days, he found that he had a sick Lee on his hands. Until now, the three Americans had suffered their share of frostbitten noses and fingers. But, with the travel going so well, they had looked on these hardships as minor annoyances. Now, however, Lee seemed a little too ill for comfort.

Peary had no idea of what was wrong with the young man. But, at the end of a day's march, he looked at the pale face, gave Lee some medicine, and ordered him to rest in the tent. Lee objected, insisting that he was needed to help feed the dogs. They were ravenously hungry after the long hours in harness. Two men would never be able to feed them and keep them under control at the same time.

Still, Peary ordered Lee to the tent. But he knew that the young man was right. So did Matt. Already, sensing that dinner was at hand, the dogs were jumping about excitedly, yelping, and snapping at each other. It was an uneasy Matt who drove a series of stakes into the ice. Then he and Peary waded into the struggling mass of fur. Perspiration broke out on their faces as they freed each team from its sledge and, keeping the dogs in their traces, dragged them to the stakes and tied them down, five to eight dogs to a stake.

Once the animals were lashed in place, the jumping changed to a blind plunging and the yelping to a savage barking. For now Matt was dragging great chunks of walrus meat from Lee's sledge. He knelt on the ice and began axing them into equal shares. Peary strode from stake to stake, his whip snapping as he attempted to hold the dogs back and keep them from breaking loose.

Then, suddenly, one stake gave way. Eight dogs slithered across the ice, tumbling over each other in a kaleidoscope of fur, rolling eyes, and flashing teeth. They collected themselves in a split second, got their bearings, and headed for Matt. He jumped to one side as, with traces flying, they swept past and hurled themselves at the meat.

In the next instant, wherever Matt looked, there was pandemonium. The staked dogs were straining and plunging in a frenzy. Everywhere, stakes broke in half or popped out of the ice. Forty-two dogs came charging and all met in one giant crash. They knocked sledges and supply crates out of the way en route. In the battle that followed, they snapped at anything in sight—each other, the traces, every last scrap of meat underfoot.

Matt and Peary, using their whip handles as clubs, tried to restore some order. But they gave up quickly. There was too much danger of being bitten or of having their furs ripped by those savage teeth. The two men darted to safety. They shrugged with the understanding that they could do nothing but wait for the dogs to finish off the meat, regardless of whether each got a fair share.

When it was all over and the dogs were quiet again, the drudgery of untangling the traces had to be faced. It was a job that took five hours. At one point in the work, Matt suddenly looked up with a frown. After all the days of calm weather, a stiff wind had come from nowhere. He walked to the thermometer that was mounted on Peary's sledge. The temperature had plunged to 25° below zero. Kokoyah at last was sending a storm.

It struck in another two days. One of the worse winds that Matt had ever experienced came screaming down the ice—with "express-train speed," Peary later wrote. The men quickly put up a tent, crawled into it, and remained there for forty-eight hours. All the while, the wind raged with such force that the tent walls were flattened right down on them. Peary could hardly free himself from the pressing canvas whenever it came time to worm his way outside for fresh supplies.

Once the storm passed, the rigors of the journey truly began to take their toll. Living on biscuit and frozen reindeer meat, the men grew weaker by the day; by late April, Peary felt that they were operating at about 50 percent of full strength. They knew that they must try to eat the reindeer meat, even though it provided little nourishment. But it was rock-hard and they could only bite away tiny chunks. They tried softening the stuff in hot tea. But then, raw and dripping, it looked so nauseating that they couldn't get it down.

Of the three, Lee was in the poorest shape. He continued to be ill and he had frozen that troublesome toe again. The pain was so great that Peary wanted him to ride on a sledge. But Lee refused. He said that he didn't want to be a bigger burden than he already was.

Making matters worse for everyone was the altitude. Ever since coming onto the icecap, they had been steadily moving upwards to the summit that, like a giant spine, ran the full length of Greenland and divided the country roughly into two halves. Now, with April coming to an end, they were at an elevation of 7,600 feet and close to the summit. In the thin, cold air, they had to fight for every breath.

Matt found that he really didn't have too much trouble when he walked at a steady pace. But if he had to stop to tie a boot lace or pick up a dropped mitten—then he was in trouble. For then he had to run to catch up with his sledge. Within a few steps, he was gasping helplessly and sometimes his nose was bleeding.

Life was no easier for the sledges and the dogs. The sledges were being ripped to pieces by the razor-sharp *sastrugi* and had to be repaired again and again. As for the dogs, they grew weaker and more exhausted with each day. Almost daily, one would drop dead in his traces or be found curled lifeless in the snow at the end of a night's encampment. The supply of walrus meat ran out at month's end and, to keep the teams going, Peary was forced to kill the weakest animals and feed them to the strongest. Only seventeen of the forty-two dogs were left by early May. Death reduced their number to eleven in the next days.

The explorers did all they could to help the animals. They lightened the sledges by removing all extra equipment and throwing it away. Sledges were abandoned as soon as their loads became small enough to be transferred to other rigs. Often, on particularly difficult stretches of ice, the men got into harness and pulled right along with the teams.

The trio reached the summit of the icecap in the first week of May and started down the eastern side. Once again, except for a hard wind, the weather was good. Peary said that they were now 500 miles out from Anniversary Lodge. Soon—very soon—they'd reach the end of the cap and enter the brown and rocky land that he and Astrup had explored in 1892. Throughout the next days, Matt constantly peered ahead for some glimpse of that land. But, with his eyes burning from five weeks of living with glaring ice, he could see nothing. Then—

Up went Peary's hand in the signal to halt. Matt braked his sledge and hurried to the explorer. In a moment, Lee joined them. The three men stood together while Peary pointed into the distance—pointed to what

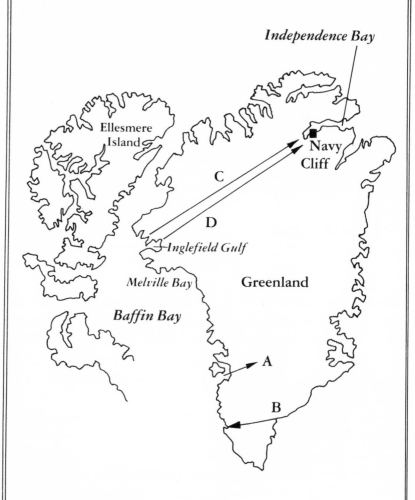

A   Peary—1886

B   Nansen—1888

C   Peary—1892

D   Peary, Matt, and Lee—1895

seemed to be a bluish smudge. That smudge, he said, was mountainous land. Somewhere in its midst were Navy Cliff and Independence Bay.

A wave of triumph surged through Matt. He could feel the same emotion pouring out of his companions. They had beaten the icecap and the victory shone in their faces. Matt looked from one to the other. He had never seen such faces in his life. Both Peary and Lee looked like wild men. Their eyes were bloodshot and pulled down at the corners with exhaustion. Their beards were long, coated over with ice. Their cheeks were torn open where the skin had been frozen again and again. He touched his own face and knew that it was as battered and pulped as theirs.

They had won out over the icecap. But they were starving and so weak and tired that they could barely stand. What next?

4.

Matt found out at the end of that day's march, which brought them down close to the edge of the icecap. Looming now in the distance were the mountains north of Independence Bay. Peary remembered the musk oxen that he and Astrup had shot in a valley while marching toward those mountains. He hoped now that there would be musk oxen, or some other kind of game, closer at hand. He told Matt that the two of them were going hunting.

Leaving Lee behind to care for the dogs, they dropped off the edge of the icecap for what turned out to be a very frustrating two days. In all that time, while Lee watched them through binoculars from above, they sighted not one oxen. Not one wolf or hare. Not even one small ptarmigan.

Disappointed, they returned to the cap. There, it was agreed that no more time should be wasted hunting in the immediate neighborhood. It would be best to push on toward Independence Bay and hope to sight some musk oxen along the way. Perhaps in the valley where Peary and Astrup had once had such good luck.

The decision made, Peary led the way down to the tumbled land that, strewn with rocks, now tore at their boots and sledges and bloodied the dogs' paws. Aside from an eight-pound hare that Matt shot, there was no game to be seen in the next days. Even the valley of the musk oxen, when at last it came into view, lay empty of life. But, in a valley just beyond it, Matt felt a surge of hope.

For there, sprinkled over the ground, were oxen tracks, all freshly made! Again, Lee was left behind with the dogs. Armed each with a rifle, Matt and Peary moved quietly forward. They followed the tracks clear across the valley, finally halting to crouch in the shelter of a great boulder. Up ahead was the most heartening sight they had seen in weeks.

About 200 yards away, on the side of a low hill, there were twenty-odd musk oxen. The animals were apparently enjoying a midday rest. A number of cows and their calves were lying down. Nearby, a great bull was wandering back and forth, as if casually on guard.

Both men stared hungrily at the small herd. But they dared not risk a shot from this distance. They were too weak and trembling to trust their aim. Under no circumstances must they miss and send the animals running to safety. This was no hunt for sport, but for survival. They must, Peary said, move up until they were within easy range. So that there wouldn't be the time to pick up their scent, they'd have to rush the hillside.

Long afterwards, Peary remembered and recorded their conversation, how Matt nodded and asked what the oxen would do when they sighted the intruders. "Do you think they will come at us, sir?"

"God knows, I hope so." With the oxen charging straight at them, they couldn't miss. Peary took a breath. "Are you ready?"

"Yes, sir."

"Come on, then."

As one, the hunters jumped up and swept around the boulder. They were sighted immediately. "There was a snort and a stamp from the big bull guarding the herd," Peary later wrote, "and the next instant every animal was facing us; the next, they were in a close line with lowered heads and horns."

Peary could have "yelled for joy." They were going to charge and "I knew now that we were sure of some of them."

Then: "We were within less than fifty yards of the herd, when the big bull with a quick motion lowered his horns still more. Instinct, Providence, call it what you will, told me it was the signal for the herd to charge. Without slackening my pace, I pulled my Winchester to my shoulder, and sent a bullet at the back of his neck . . ."

The bull sank to its haunches. The herd, suddenly frightened, wavered as if to break and run for safety. "A cow half turned, and as Matt's rifle cracked, fell with a bullet back of her fore shoulder. Without raising my rifle above my hips, another one dropped. Then another, for Matt . . ."

Now the animals did turn. They fled up the hillside, heading for a low ridge. Once across it and out of sight, they would scatter and be gone. Running now on rising ground, Peary saw a wounded cow wheel just above him. She lowered her head, ready to charge the explorer. But Matt's rifle cracked and she fell. Peary heard Matt shout, "My last cartridge!"

The herd was disappearing over the ridge. Peary glimpsed a last shaggy hulk silhouetted against the sky. Without taking aim, but depending on instinct alone, he fired a final shot. The animal staggered and then dropped.

Suddenly, all was quiet again. The hunt was over. But now the feast began. Matt hurried back for Lee and the dogs. Then the men spent the hours from late afternoon to midnight skinning the oxen. As they worked, and not even bothering to light a campfire, they downed great bites of the warm, raw meat and doled out generous chunks to the teams. For everyone—man and animal alike—it was the first fully nourishing meal in weeks.

In the next days, as the party continued northeast toward the approaching mountains, Peary bagged several more musk oxen. By the time

Independence Bay burst into view in mid-May, the sledges were packed with the meat of six fully grown oxen and four calves. No one would starve to death on the way home.

It was an awestruck Matt who stood with Peary at the edge of Navy Cliff. Four thousand feet below him lay the ice-choked waters of the Bay. Off to his right was Academy Glacier. And there, looming in the north beyond the Bay, were the mountains—those mountains that seemed to be islands stretching away into the Arctic Ocean. This moment of drinking in the wild beauty all around made all the starvation and hardship of past weeks seem worthwhile.

He heard Peary describe the work that must be done. Though a probe northward from here had always been intended, Peary now felt that a hike across the Bay to the distant mountains was out of the question; though refreshed by the oxen meat, his men were still too weak and exhausted for such an effort. The best that they could hope to do was find a route down from these great heights to the Bay. Then, on a future expedition, he'd push off from there in quest of the mountains and the Pole beyond.

The search for a route down to the Bay turned the triumph of reaching the northeast corner into a disaster. Everywhere they turned, they met with failure. No matter where they hiked—along moraines, down slopes, or through ravines—they always ended at a sheer drop to the water far below. Daily, Matt saw Peary's face grow more deeply lined with worry. And then defeat, when the explorer had to admit a terrible truth.

There *was no route* down to the Bay—at least, not one that he would ever find. Ever since 1892, he had thought of those distant mountains as stepping-stones to the Pole. They might well be. But he would never know because he'd never be able to reach them. He had wasted three years—and risked many lives—to come back here and learn that bitter truth. With the learning, the dream of reaching the North Pole from the northeast corner of Greenland came to a sudden and heartbreaking end.

Peary had just turned thirty-nine years old. But he looked more than twice that age when he faced his men and said that the work was done. All three were exhausted from the days of searching. The sledges were in tatters. Only nine dogs were still alive. No more time could be spent here. While they still had a shadow of strength left, they must start for home.

Matt and Lee had never seen the explorer look more crushed than when he led them back across the icecap. Both knew he thought himself a complete failure. Both knew that he couldn't bear the thought of returning to the United States as such. Lee watched him with deep concern during the crossing of an area webbed with crevasses hidden just beneath the ice. The man forged ahead swiftly, almost blindly. Lee felt that he was hoping to stumble into one of those hidden abysses and end forever the need to go home.

As for Matt, his feelings were mixed. On the one hand, he sorrowed for Peary in defeat. But, on the other, he knew his man. Peary, once he was strong again, would regain his old vigor. The ambition to reach the North Pole would burn again just as brightly as ever. He'd go right on questing after that great prize by looking for a new route there. Matt was sure of it.

For himself, Matt felt a deep pride. He had faced every challenge that the icecap had to offer. He'd beaten them all and had become the first black man ever to cross Greenland. He had proven himself an explorer.

In the years to come, when Peary came north again, Matt Henson would be with him, surely as a full-fledged assistant this time and not merely as a servant.

8. The North Pole
1898-1900

To the Arctic Ocean

THE three men made their way back to Anniversary Lodge in twenty-four days of steady marching that used up most of their supplies and their last reserves of strength. On their arrival in late June, they were weak and starving. They had barely the strength left to push open the Lodge door.

Fed by the Eskimos, the trio spent July resting and slowly regaining their strength. But so slowly that Peary wondered if they'd ever be able to sledge down the west coast in search of a whaler to take them home. As matters turned out, the trip never had to be made. Startled, the explorer awoke from a nap on August 3 to find Jo's brother, Emil Diebitsch, standing over him.

Even before Peary was fully awake, Diebitsch was saying that he had come north with the *Kite*, that sturdy little veteran of the 1891-92 expedition, to fetch Peary home. He explained that Jo, desperately worried about her husband, had spent the last months trying to raise enough money to charter the ship. She'd collected some funds through a series of lectures on her Arctic adventures. The rest had come from a wealthy businessman who had long admired Peary and his work—Morris K. Jesup, President of the American Museum of Natural History.

Though happy to be going home to Jo and little Marie, it was a troubled Peary who sailed away from Anniversary Lodge. He'd stayed in Greenland an extra year to make a success of his expedition; but now, having been unable to probe north from Navy Cliff, he still considered himself a failure. And so he had the *Kite* stop just off a desolate beach in Melville Bay. He was remembering the three meteorites that he and Lee had visited there. If he could take them back for display in the American Museum of Natural History, at least he wouldn't be returning empty-handed.

During the stop, Matt watched Peary become an engineer again. Helped by the ship's crew and some Eskimos, the explorer dug the earth away from the "woman" and the "dog," lifted them from their frozen beds with hydraulic jacks, and eased them onto sledgelike transports made of spruce poles. The men got each sledge down to the water's edge by pushing it along a series of iron rollers placed crossways in its path. Then the meteorites were placed on a giant floe and ferried out to the *Kite*, there to be swung aboard with ropes and winch.

Weighing 5,500 pounds and 1,000 pounds respectively, the "woman" and the "dog" proved relatively easy to move. But, on its island out in the bay, the "tent" refused to budge. Peary gauged its weight to be around 90 tons, and the jacks simply couldn't handle it. He said that he'd have to come back for it with superior equipment at a later date.

Matt didn't see the struggle with the "tent" because he was busy with a special assignment. Several walrus had been shot and Peary wanted to take their hides home as a presentation to the Museum. Thanks to the special training that Matt had received from the Eskimos, the job of skinning the animals went to him.

It turned out to be an important assignment for Matt. When the *Kite* anchored at New York City in September, the curator of the Museum came aboard to view the meteorites and the hides. He was especially impressed with the way the hides had been handled. On learning that Matt had done the work, he promptly offered him a job in the Museum's taxidermy department.

And, just as promptly, Matt accepted. As was usual between expeditions, Peary couldn't afford to employ him any longer and he had been wondering where he could find work. He reported to the Museum a few weeks later and—except for two brief Greenland visits with Peary—remained there until 1898. His job called for him to assist in the preparation of animals for mounting.

After a warm welcome from his family, Peary returned to his Navy duties. In the summer of 1896, he took time off to sail to Melville Bay with Matt and Lee in an effort to collect the "tent." Heavy ice kept them from reaching their destination, forcing them to try again in the summer of 1897. This time, with heavy hydraulic jacks, they freed the meteorite, lowered it down a slope to the water's edge with ropes, and then hoisted it aboard their ship.

It was an engineering feat that marked Lee's final work with Peary. On the return to the United States, he went home for good, always to remember the explorer with warmth and admiration. As for the "tent," it was put on display at the American Museum of Natural History, along with the "woman" and the "dog." Years later, Peary sold the three meteorites to the Museum for $40,000. The sale earned him widespread criticism.

Many people felt that he had no right to deprive the Eskimos of a precious source of metal. Peary replied that whalers were by now visiting Baffin Bay regularly and supplying the Eskimos with a variety of metal tools and weapons. The Eskimos no longer needed the meteorites.

Though Peary had been disappointed when he couldn't reach the "tent" in 1896, he came home to some good news. At last, after all the months of worried waiting, there was word of the Nansen expedition. The Norwegian had just returned with the announcement that he had failed to reach the North Pole.

Matt was at work in the Museum when he heard the news. He could imagine how Peary must be sighing with relief. The great dream of the explorer's life was still alive.

But the newspapers told Matt that the Norwegian had come very close to his goal. On departing Norway back in 1893, Nansen had sailed into the Arctic Ocean and had allowed his ship to become locked in the ice pack above Russia. For months, he'd drifted aimlessly until he found himself inching steadily northward and realized that he had picked up his suspected current. Then, throughout 1894, he had followed an arcing path across the Arctic Ocean, all the while drawing nearer to the Pole.

By year's end, however, he knew that the path would never carry him right across the crown of the world. With the Pole still some 400 miles away, the current started to swing south toward a point in the Atlantic Ocean between Greenland and the Spitzbergen Islands. In an attempt not to be cheated of the great prize, Nansen went over the side and made a sledge run toward the Pole. He came to within about 225 miles of his destination before the rough ice defeated him.

Matt breathed deeply. That was close. *Very* close.

He knew that, ever since leaving Anniversary Lodge, Peary had been thinking about his next trip north, the one that would see him head for the Pole via another route. Now, with Nansen out of the way, he wondered how the plan was developing.

2.

Matt found out at the end of the 1897 summer voyage. While sailing home with the "tent," Peary called him to his cabin, unrolled a map of Greenland, and pointed to the far northern area.

There, some miles above Inglefield Gulf, Baffin Bay narrowed down and finally ended, turning into a series of water passages that speared northward and at last opened into the Arctic Ocean. The passages cut their way between Greenland and Ellesmere Island, which was the northernmost of a clutter of islands—known as the Northwest Territorials—above Canada. On his fingers, Peary ticked off the passages as they ran from south to north: Smith Sound, Kane Basin, Kennedy Channel, and Robeson Channel.

Peary said that he planned to force a ship up through those ice-choked passages. On reaching the Arctic Ocean, he'd establish a base camp on the north coast of either Greenland or Ellesmere Island, whichever seemed the more inviting. Then, from that camp, he'd launch his attempts to sledge over the frozen sea to the North Pole, more than 400 miles away.

Matt blinked. Attempts? Peary nodded. It would be fine, he said, if he managed to make his way all across the rough, shifting ice on his first try. But, if not, he intended to remain there in the Arctic, trying again and again until he succeeded.

Each attempt, he went on, would be made in the daylight months of the year. Failure would see him winter at the base camp, living off Arctic game and his supplies while he readied himself for a new assault the following year. He was ready to remain in the Arctic for as long as four years.

Matt had to fight to keep his mouth from dropping open as he listened. Without a doubt, this was the most daring and ambitious plan that the explorer had ever concocted. Four years in the Arctic! Without ever the relief of coming home to rest. It was a staggering thought.

So staggering, indeed, that it caused Matt to hesitate when Peary asked if he would come along as an assistant. Matt was now thirty-one years old. He had a good job at the Museum. If he went north for those many years, what would he do when he came back? Surely, the Museum wouldn't wait for him that long. Would he have to go wandering from one menial job to another, as he had done as a young man?

But he shrugged his fears aside. Other thoughts came crowding into mind and made a distant and cloudy future seem unimportant. If he could help Peary reach the North Pole, he would bring great honor to black people everywhere and help to show the world that they were fit for far better work than most of them were now allowed to do.

And—for the first time a dream of his own took shape—if he could travel all the way across the Arctic Ocean with Peary, then he would match the explorer's magnificent feat. He would become the first black man ever to stand at the roof of the world.

He nodded. Of course, he'd come along.

In the next months, as he worked at the Museum, Matt kept track of Peary's preparations. He knew when the explorer, over the objections of many officers who felt he'd been given too much time off already, received a five-year leave from the Navy to continue his work; though he planned to be away only four years, Peary asked for five, in case the extra time was needed. Matt knew when a wealthy friend donated a ship to the expedition. And he knew when Morris K. Jesup, who had helped send the *Kite* to Anniversary Lodge, organized the Peary Arctic Club. Its membership was made up of wealthy men who were willing to provide Peary with funds. Thanks to their help—and to that of other friends and admirers—the explorer was spared long months of looking for money.

And so it was that, in the summer of 1898, Matt left his job at the Museum and once again sailed up Baffin Bay with Peary. Because the expedition was to be away for so long, only one other man was coming along as an assistant. He was Dr. T. S. Dedrick, whose services as a physician would be needed. All other help would come from the ship's crew and from the Greenland Eskimos. Even Jo was being left behind.

For as long as he lived, Matt would never forget how Peary and Jo looked at the moment of their farewell. Their faces had been tight with suppressed emotion and they had remained clasped in each other's arms for a long moment, knowing that it might be years before they saw each other again. Then Jo had given her husband a parting gift—an American flag that she had sewn of red, white, and blue taffeta. She had asked him to carry it always as a reminder that she was at his side in spirit. From that day on, wherever Peary sledged in the Arctic, the flag went with him, inside his jacket, close to his heart.

Watching, Matt had marveled at Jo. In letting her husband go in search of his lifelong dream, even if it meant a separation of years, she struck Matt as possibly the most courgeous and unselfish woman he had ever met.

3.

Matt knew that the passages north from Baffin Bay would be crowded with ice. But, as soon as the expedition's ship, *Windward*, pushed through Smith Sound in August and entered Kane Basin, he shook his head. The Basin wasn't just crowded with ice. It was literally choked with it.

Back at Cape York, the expedition had anchored for a time to hire twenty Eskimo sledge drivers and their teams. Now, for five long days in a row, Matt stood at the ship's rail with the drivers and watched the *Windward* push her way into any lane of open water that presented itself. But then there were no more leads. And no more progress. The Eskimos began to point in all directions. A vast field of sometimes flat and sometimes jumbled white had completely circled the ship. She was stuck fast.

The Eskimos were quick to say that, with the bad months just ahead, there seemed no chance that the ice would break up and permit the *Windward* to advance. Unless the gods gave Peary a miracle, he was trapped here for the winter.

It was a grim prediction. For a time, Matt and the explorer hoped that it wouldn't come true. But, by October, they knew the Eskimos were right. The ice wasn't going to budge, not even enough to give them the slightest passage forward. They were stalled 300 miles south of the Arctic Ocean. The plan to reach the sea this year so that a Pole run could be launched next spring was dead.

But no, Peary said suddenly. There was still a chance. The *Windward* lay just off the coast of Ellesmere Island. On that island, some 250 miles north of their position, was a place called Fort Conger. It was no more than a cabin that had been built in the early 1880s by the American explorer, Adolphus W. Greely, during an ill-fated attempt to reach the Pole, an attempt that had ended with seventeen of his twenty-three men dead of starvation . . .

Matt saw the point immediately. If the cabin was still standing after all these years, Peary could use it as a base camp. From there, come spring, he could sledge the remaining miles to the Arctic Ocean and launch the Pole run as scheduled. Matt heard Peary order him to prepare for the trip to Conger.

Matt always remembered the next weeks as some of the worst in his Arctic career. To prepare for the trip, he had to do more than just load the sledges with supplies and put them over the side. Before the rigs dared move north, he had to pickaxe a trail for them. Why?

Because the ice here was far different from the kind up on the Greenland cap. Though bad enough on the cap, at least it had been unmoving and relatively smooth. But here, it was being constantly pushed and shoved by a restless sea. As the pack crunched against Ellesmere Island, it smashed itself into a nightmare of tumbled white. Floes came pressing together and rose in towering, jagged pressure ridges. Joining them were great blocks of ice—called hummocks—that were pushed up on end or that climbed atop each other to heights of fifty feet. Without a trail that smoothed the way over or around all these obstacles, the supply sledges could never hope to reach Conger.

Matt and a team of six Eskimos chopped their way north as the winter dark fell. By December, they were back at the ship with the news that the trail was cut halfway to the fort. Matt now expected to remain aboard the *Windward* until February. Then, when there was again daylight to see by, the remaining miles could be carved out and the supplies could be moved forward in time for the springtime run to the Pole.

But he stared in astonishment. For Peary had other ideas. The supplies must be sledged forward immediately—all the way to Conger! In the winter dark? Yes. Not a moment must be lost in taking possession of the fort.

Peary explained the reasons for his hurry. Back in the United States, when he'd heard of Nansen's failure to reach the Pole, he had thought that he now had the field all to himself. But, just before he'd started north, the newspapers had reported that another Norwegian—Otto Sverdrup—was planning a voyage identical to his own. Quite by coincidence, Sverdrup was heading for the same four passages as he, with the aim of anchoring at Greenland's northern coast for a try at the Pole. Throughout the journey up Baffin Bay, Peary had kept watch for Sverdrup and had been relieved to see no sign of him. But . . .

While Matt had been cutting the trail, Peary had used the time to explore the southern area of Ellesmere Island. And there, he had stumbled upon Sverdrup, who said that he was camped nearby, with his ship stopped by ice farther south. Peary had returned to the *Windward*, certain that Sverdrup must know of Fort Conger. He was afraid that the Norwegian might be planning to head there and use it as an advance base. Peary must get there ahead of him and claim the fort for himself.

And so, in late December, Matt was out on the ice again, with Peary and Dr. Dedrick coming up behind him with the supply sledges and their Eskimo drivers. The sledges bumped over the trail and then moved forward in a series of stops and starts while Matt, finding that the worst ice was behind him, quickly hacked out a path over the remaining miles to Conger. In mid-January, 1899, he found the cabin still standing and became the first man in more than fifteen years to push its front door open.

The journey and the work of trailblazing had left him exhausted and wondering what the ice would be like out on the Arctic Ocean. Would it be worse than the tumbled nightmare that lay between here and the *Windward*? If so, how would the expedition ever manage to struggle across several hundred miles of it to the North Pole?

But, as exhausted as Matt was, he was in better shape than Peary. The explorer was pleased to find the cabin usable and Sverdrup nowhere in sight, but his face was drawn with worry when he entered. Matt heard him tell Dedrick that he had a "strange wooden feeling" in his legs. The doctor, knowing one of the prime signs of frostbite when he heard it, immediately cut Peary's boots away. Then the men in the room, Americans and Eskimos alike, stared in silent horror at the explorer's feet.

Water had gotten into Peary's boots out on the trail and had frozen solid all about his feet. Both feet—dead white but with the toes purple with unmoving blood—were frostbitten. The circulation had been stopped for hours and gangrene, a decaying of the tissues, was forming on the toes. To keep the decay from spreading, Dedrick was forced to amputate small portions of seven toes. As he worked by the light of Matt's alcohol lamp, the doctor was certain that he'd be operating again soon.

Everyone knew immediately that the springtime run was now out of the question. Dedrick told Matt that Peary should be taken back to the *Windward* right away so that better care could be given him. But a series of storms pinned the men down where they were for four weeks. At last, with the sky clearing in February, and the sun rising for the first time in 1899, Matt settled Peary aboard a sledge for the journey south. For the next eleven days, he watched the explorer silently clamping his teeth against the pain that went shooting through him with every bump in the trail.

On arriving at the ship, Dr. Dedrick did what he had always known he must do. The gangrene was still spreading. He amputated all of Peary's toes except the two small ones.

Throughout the operation, Matt paced the deck outside, his mind a welter of bleak thoughts. All of Peary's bad luck of old had come rushing back to haunt the man. He had defied the winter to claim his advance camp, but what good had it done him? With practically all his toes gone, he could never hope to make his way across the vicious Arctic Ocean ice. Not in the spring. Not ever.

For a moment, Matt felt that he was back aboard the *Kite* eight years ago. He heard himself murmuring the words that Dr. Cook had said after setting the explorer's broken leg:

You'll have to go home.

But, this time, it would be for good. No more Arctic work. No more great dreams of the North Pole.

4.

In the next weeks, Matt went right on thinking that he was back aboard the *Kite*. As before, Peary refused to hear any talk of quitting and heading for home. He was still going to the North Pole. Eight missing toes weren't going to stop him. He acknowledged that he wouldn't be fit for the journey this year. But he'd be ready by the spring of 1900.

Then, over the protests of Dr. Dedrick, he got back to the business of exploring. Without waiting for his feet to heal, he climbed aboard a sledge and rode over to Ellesmere Island to chart its southern area. By July, he was walking with the aid of crutches. He told everyone that he was doing fine, but he admitted in his diary that the pain of moving about on the hard, rough ice was great, especially in his right foot.

In August, after holding her prisoner for a year, the ice in Kane Basin finally broke up and released the *Windward*. The ship immediately retreated down to Baffin Bay. There, three pieces of good news lay in store for Peary.

First, he found a small ship waiting for him at the Eskimo settlement of Etah on Greenland's coast. Her name was *Diana* and she had come north with additional supplies from Morris K. Jesup and the Peary Arctic Club. Second, there were letters from home aboard, among them a particularly important one from Jo. Peary read that he and his wife had become the parents of another daughter—Francine, born in January while he was at Fort Conger.

Finally, there was good news about Otto Sverdrup. After months in the Ellesmere area, the Norwegian had decided the ice was still so bad that he would never be able to force his ship up the four passages to the

Arctic Ocean. He'd abandoned his plan to try for the Pole and had moved off to explore elsewhere. Once again, the field was left to Peary.

Peary felt that he, too, would never get a ship up the passages at present, and so he sent the *Windward* and the *Diana* home to the United States in September, saying that from here on he would depend on sledges. Then, after wintering at Etah and tossing his crutches aside, he marched north to Conger with Matt, Dedrick, and the Eskimo drivers. They arrived at the cabin in March, 1900. Matt, who had been worried about Peary's feet all during the trek, was pleased when the explorer said that, though they still bothered him, he could now walk with "reasonable comfort."

Peary went on to say that he had reached a decision about the start of the Pole run. From Conger, they could now either strike out for Elles- mere's northernmost coast or cross over to Greenland and launch the run from there. Peary said that he had opted for the latter. If the Arctic Ocean ice managed to prevent a run this year, then he could chart Green- land's northern coast and add to his proof that the country was a vast island.

The decision made, Peary and Matt left Dedrick in charge of the cabin and sledged across Robeson Channel—the northernmost of the passages —with their Eskimo drivers. They proceeded north along the Greenland coast in April, reached the Arctic Ocean, and began following the shore northeast. They were searching for the most northerly tip of land from which they could jump off for the Pole, and the trip was a harrowing one.

Matt exhausted himself pickaxing a trail through ice as rough as that on the road to Conger. The Eskimos were nervous the whole time and always talking about running away; they hated to be here on the edge of the frozen ocean; this was the kingdom of Tornarsuk, the greatest of all the northern devils; he'd treat Peary far worse than Kokoyah did up on the icecap. As for Peary himself, he was no longer walking with "rea- sonable comfort."

His feet kept striking obstacles in the ice and the pain was so great at times that it made him sick to his stomach. Further, the pain shot up his legs and weakened them. Only after about 300 miles of travel did his legs again seem strong enough to support him. By that time, he had developed a way of walking that gave his feet some comfort. Rather than taking ordinary steps, he slid forward in a kind of shuffle. It was a method that he used for as long as he remained in the Arctic.

Matt continued to lead the way northeast through April, passing northern points reached back in the 1880s by two of Greely's explorers. Then, in May, he arrived at a cape and saw that, beyond it, the coast began to dip southeast. Peary was sure—correctly so—that this was Greenland's northernmost point. He named the cape in honor of Morris K. Jesup.

Then, in an action that was to become touchingly familiar to Matt in the next years, Peary removed a package from inside his jacket. Out came the American flag that Jo had sewn of taffeta. He cut two small pieces from it—one from the field of stars, the other from the striped area. They were placed in a rock cairn, to be left behind in memory of his visit to this desolate and far northern spot.

Peary looked at his men. He knew that they—not to mention himself, with his battered feet—were too worn for a serious run at the Pole. That would have to wait for next year. But he did decide on a test run over the ice. It was a hike that took the party fifteen miles out to sea, where they were stopped by a lane of open water. A solar observation showed them to be at a latitude of 83° 50′ North. It was the farthest north that Peary and Matt had ever traveled.

On returning to Cape Jesup, the party continued southeast, at last reaching an offshore island—today known as Wyckoff—on May 22. They were 400 miles from Conger, Peary said, and this was surely the far northeastern tip of Greenland. Nothing but ocean could be seen to the north, east, and southeast. But, when he turned southwest, he could glimpse through the mists a distant mountain that he recognized as having sighted while he stood gazing north from Navy Cliff in 1895.

The explorer was elated. He hadn't made it to the Pole. That was yet to come. But, so far as geographers everywhere would be concerned, he'd done something quite as important. More than in his past trips, he had shown Greenland to be a vast island.

He turned to Matt and said it was time to return to Conger. Matt saw the satisfaction in Peary's face and felt it reflected in his own. Peary had proven that Greenland was an island. But the proof had been won with the help of a black man. It was an honor that Matt would quietly carry for his people for the rest of his life.

He swung westward. Already, he was thinking about next year's work.

9. The North Pole
1901-1909

Across the Frozen Sea

WHEN the party arrived back at Fort Conger on June 10, 1900, Matt could see that he had a very confident Peary on his hands. Though the explorer had always been ready to try for the Pole at the first opportunity, he obviously now felt better prepared for the effort than ever before. The exploration of Greenland's northern coast had been a rehearsal that had taught him two important lessons.

First, he'd learned much about the problems of sledging over the tossed and shifting sea ice, ice that was so different from the type up on the icecap. Second, he'd realized that he must now keep his expeditions supplied in a different way.

On the icecap, his men had been able to cache supplies for him months ahead of time. That system would never work on the sea ice. Caches could be put down for hours or a few days, but not for months. They'd float away with the current and be irretrievably lost.

And so, from now on, he would have to use more men than he had once thought wise. He would divide them into what he called divisions or supporting parties. Made up of several heavily laden sledges each, the divisions would keep him provisioned as he moved north. As the sledges were emptied, they would be sent back to base camp. Returning with them would be the most exhausted of the men. Finally, when he was approaching the last lap of his journey, he would select a handful of the strongest remaining men and they would accompany him on a final dash to the Pole. Everyone else would go back to base camp with the last empty supply sledges.

Matt was glad to see the confidence. Perhaps it would help Peary overcome the bad luck that had always dogged him. But, in the next years, Matt watched it shaken again and again as the explorer's every attempt to gain the North Pole ended in failure.

The first failure came in 1901, after a quiet winter spent at Conger. Rather than cross over to Greenland this time, Peary decided to jump off from Cape Hecla on Ellesmere's northern coast. He split Matt, Dedrick, and the Eskimo drivers into two divisions and sledged away from the cabin in early April. Eight days and ninety hard miles later, he arrived at Hecla and knew with a groan that he could go no farther. The offshore ice was too jumbled and piled too high ever to be crossed this year.

Peary was disappointed, but not overly alarmed, for he still had another year in which to make the run before his four-year Arctic stay came to an end. He retreated south to Baffin Bay and, as he had expected, found the *Windward* waiting at Etah with fresh supplies from Morris K. Jesup and the Peary Arctic Club. To his delight, he came aboard to see Jo and little Marie standing there with outstretched arms.

The reunion was a happy one, but it was marred by the sad news that baby Francine had fallen ill back home and had died at seven months of age.

It was the 1902 run that really first shattered Peary's confidence. After the *Windward* unloaded its supplies and turned for home with Jo and Marie, Peary wintered at Etah. In April, he and his men were back at Hecla. The offshore ice looked as vicious and as impassable as before. But there was no turning back this time. With Matt leading the way and pickaxing a trail, the divisions jolted their way down from the Cape. No sooner had they reached the frozen sea than they were in trouble.

And they remained in trouble for fifteen exhausting days. First, Matt found himself working in a maze of hummocks and pressure ridges. Most were so big that there wasn't a hope of cutting a trail through them. The sledges had to be picked up and lifted across some. Others—the true giants—had to be skirted. Matt spent hours wandering in one direction and then the other while he searched for ways around the obstacles.

Next, there was a stretch of flat ice, but it was covered with a layer of snow so thick that the dogs sank up to their necks in it; now it was the animals that had to be picked up and carried forward, with the men then ploughing back to fetch the sledges. Then came a patch of thin ice; it broke beneath Peary's sledge, and the rig would have disappeared into the sea forever had not Matt and the Eskimos caught it and pulled it to safety at the last moment.

Finally, a wind came screaming in from the north and topped things off. It swept ice crystals and snow up from the surface and flung them into everyone's eyes, blinding men and dogs alike. Squinting against the biting wind, Peary watched the strength draining out of his people, saw them no longer walking but staggering and falling as they bent their bodies against the terrible wind. And he felt his own strength ebbing and the pain in his still-tender feet rising up through his legs.

Then, just ahead, he glimpsed another clutter of hummocks and pressure ridges lying across his path and stretching away endlessly from east to west. He knew instantly that his men would never be able to fight their way past this newest obstacle.

The date was April 21, 1902. It was hopeless to go on. Peary called the divisions to a halt, then managed to take a solar observation that showed his position to be 84° 16′ North latitude. He and Matt had pushed well beyond the northernmost point reached on the short hike out from Cape Morris K. Jesup in 1900. It was a new "farthest north" for them. As was becoming his custom, Peary removed Jo's American flag from inside his jacket, cut a piece from it, and left the taffeta fragment buried there in the ice. Quietly, he ordered the sledges to turn south.

As he himself turned homeward, a black depression took hold of him. For the first time in his life, he felt old and broken. He had spent four straight years in the Arctic, had accomplished some fine work, yes, but had failed miserably in his prime objective. He had the terrible feeling that he had just now come as far north as he ever would.

That night, camped in his igloo, he poured his feelings into his diary. He wrote that he was too old—he was now forty-five—for the rigors of exploration. That he couldn't do the impossible. And that the dream of all the past years was now ended.

2.

Matt saw the black depression and sensed how deep it was. He watched it cling to the man all during the trip south to Baffin Bay. It was still there when the *Windward* arrived at Etah in September to take the explorer home to the United States.

Only after the arrival in New York City did Peary's ambition and great spirit break through again. Regardless of what he had written in his diary back on the ice, he must try once more for the goal of his lifetime. He *must.* With the financial backing of Jesup and the Peary Arctic Club, he began to prepare for another expedition.

The preparations filled the years from 1903 to 1905. During that time, Peary also attended to his Navy duties and sat for tests that enabled him to be promoted to the rank of Lieutenant Commander and then Commander. He and Jo became parents for the third time when a son, Robert, Jr., was born to them in 1903.

For Matt, the years were spent as a Pullman porter with the Pennsylvania Railroad. He looked on the job as a new adventure. He smilingly told friends that he'd seen a great deal of the Arctic recently; now he was getting the chance to see something of his own country.

The job wasn't the only new adventure in his life. There was another one—one that started on an evening just after the *Windward* had docked at New York City.

He'd been invited that night to the home of his good friend George Gardner in Harlem, there to meet a number of families and tell them of his Arctic adventures. Though all the families were leaders in the Harlem community, he'd ended up remembering just one guest—the slender, attractive Lucy Ross.

Soon after being introduced, Matt found himself telling Lucy all about his Eskimo friends and their way of life. And then he learned something of her—that she was unmarried and that she worked as a clerk in a New York bank. Still in her twenties, she was one of the first black women to break through the color barrier in the city's banking business. By the time the evening ended, Matt knew that he wanted to see Lucy Ross again.

They met frequently in the next months, whenever Matt had time off from the railroad. Together, they went for walks. Often, there were picnics. Often, visits to museums and art galleries. Matt, who had long thought he was destined to be a bachelor for the rest of his days, slowly came to realize that he was in love with Lucy—and that, miracle of miracles, his love was returned.

Their romance was interrupted in mid-1905, with the word that Peary was ready to sail north again. Shyly, Matt asked if Lucy would wait for him while he was gone and then marry him on his return. He held his breath for a moment, then broke into a smile when she took his hand and nodded.

Not really believing his good fortune in finding a woman as wonderful as Lucy, Matt left his railroad job. He went down to the New York docks and boarded the *Roosevelt*, a sleek but rugged steam-and-sail ship that had been built for Peary. As soon as he stepped on deck, he met the four

Shown here taking on supplies, the Roosevelt *carried Peary and his men north for the Pole runs of 1906 and 1909.*

men who would serve with him as assistants. Of the four, two were to become his close friends—Ross Marvin and the pipe-smoking Robert A. Bartlett.

Marvin was a husky young graduate of Cornell University. Bartlett, a stocky New Foundlander who was known to everyone as Bob, was employed as captain of the *Roosevelt*. He had been first mate aboard the *Windward* and had become one of Peary's closest friends.

Bartlett and the *Roosevelt*, which had been designed to push through the ice, now did what the *Windward* had been unable to do. They maneuvered their way up the four passages above Baffin Bay, clear to the edge of the Arctic Ocean, anchoring at last off the northern Ellesmere coast. From there, the assistants and the Eskimo drivers hired back at

Bob Bartlett (right) and Peary aboard the Roosevelt. *Bartlett served as master of the ship and then blazed much of the trail north to the Pole in 1909.*

Etah, sledged the supplies over to Cape Hecla. And, from Hecla, the run to the Pole began in early March, 1906, with Matt out in front and pickaxing a trail.

Once again, Peary was destined to fail. There seemed to be delays at every step of the way, delays that saw the explorer sitting impatiently on the ice while his supplies dwindled away. He ran into storms. High winds. Rough ice. And, one after the other, lanes of open water. The worst of these leads was the one that he christened the "Big Lead."

Peary had been halted for a time in 1902 by this especially wide stretch of water. It was usually to be found, knifing endlessly east and west, near 84° North latitude, and the explorer felt certain that the ice was split here because of the restlessness of the sea above the Continental

Shelf. It now stopped him for six long days before the waters brought its southern and northern shores together and allowed him to move forward.

Because of the delays, Peary was dangerously low on supplies as he pressed on into April. By mid-month, he was telling Matt that they would never have sufficient food to reach the Pole and return. Then, on April 21—the anniversary of his 1902 defeat—he halted the sledges for the last time and ordered the divisions to turn back.

Matt stared at him and felt tears starting up behind his eyes. The expedition was clear up to 87° 6′ North. Peary had brought his men farther north than any human being had ever traveled before. They all stood just 174 miles from the top of the world. But, thanks to Peary's usual poor luck, they were 174 impossible miles.

Desperately low on supplies—so low, in fact, that the men had to kill some of the sledge dogs for food—the expedition again ran into the Big Lead, open once more, yawning from a half mile to two miles wide. With starving men on his hands and with the Eskimos ready to panic because they thought that the great devil Tornarsuk was out to kill them, Peary dared not sit and wait for the lead to close. For two days, the men searched all along it for some point where it could be crossed.

At last, they found a "bridge"—a sheet of thin young ice stretching across two miles of water to the opposite shore of white. Hardly daring to breathe, the men began to cross over, finding the ice so fragile that it rose and fell with the movement of the water underneath. They walked at fifty-foot intervals, with their legs spread wide to reduce the concentration of their weight, and with their feet sliding along so as not to poke holes in the blue-white surface. Even then, it cracked and threatened to break beneath them and the sledges time and again.

But the "bridge" held. Matt again blazed the trail as the sledgers continued south. They were almost dead of starvation when they arrived at the *Roosevelt* in late May.

Once more, Matt saw the black depression take hold of Peary. But the explorer quickly threw it aside this time. He took several weeks to ex-

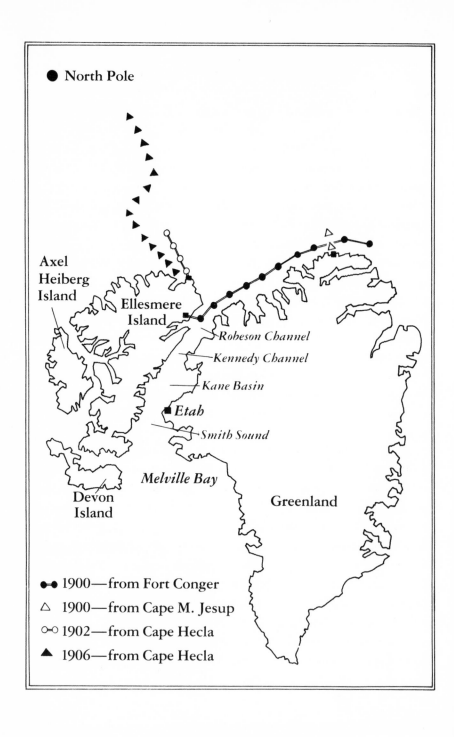

North Pole

Axel
Heiberg
Island

Ellesmere
Island

Robeson Channel

Kennedy Channel

Kane Basin

■*Etah*

Smith Sound

Melville Bay

Devon
Island

Greenland

●─● 1900—from Fort Conger
△ 1900—from Cape M. Jesup
○─○ 1902—from Cape Hecla
▲ 1906—from Cape Hecla

plore the far western reaches of Ellesmere and then, as soon as the *Roosevelt* made her way back to the United States, began to plan yet another try. Matt shook his head and wondered when the explorer would ever give up.

He gave himself an immediate answer. This next expedition had to be the last. Peary was now approaching fifty years of age. If he didn't win this time, he'd simply be too old to keep on trying. And Matt knew that he himself, now forty, couldn't go on forever either, no matter how much he wanted to help Peary, and no matter how much he dreamed of being the first black man at the Pole. Neither of them was made of iron. They were both flesh and blood, like everyone else in the world.

The expedition took shape in 1907. For a time that year, Matt put aside all thoughts of the Arctic. He and Lucy Ross were married on a warm day in September. But soon Matt's eyes were turned north again. He was aboard the *Roosevelt* when the ship sailed out of New York in July of 1908.

As he stood at the rail waving good-bye to his new wife, there were five assistants on deck with him. Heading the list were the veterans Bob Bartlett and Ross Marvin. The remaining three were Arctic rookies. They were: Dr. J. W. Goodsell of Pennsylvania, the expedition's physician; Donald Macmillan, a fine athlete and a teacher at Worcester Academy in Massachusetts; and George Borup, a recent Yale graduate. At twenty-one, Borup was the "baby" of the group. The others ranged from the late twenties to early thirties.

As usual, Peary stopped at Etah to hire some Eskimo help. About two dozen drivers, workers, and their families and teams came aboard. A delighted Matt saw that, among the Eskimos willing to challenge Tornarsuk's domain, was his "adopted son" Kudlooktoo, now grown from a button-eyed little boy to a muscular young man. The two were overjoyed when Peary said that Kudlooktoo could cross the Arctic Ocean as a member of Matt's division.

Troubling news, however, awaited Peary at Etah. It concerned his old

Dr. J. W. Goodsell,
physician for the 1909
expedition.

friend from the Red Cliff days—Dr. Frederick A. Cook. Ever since that first Greenland visit, the doctor had been interested in Polar exploration. He'd served with an expedition in the Antarctic and, just last year, had returned to northern Greenland, saying that he was on a hunting trip. Now, at Etah, Peary learned that Cook and a band of Eskimos were exploring somewhere in the Ellesmere Island area and that he had been talking about heading for the North Pole himself.

Even before he'd left New York, Peary had heard this rumor from friends who knew Cook and suspected that the real purpose behind his "hunting trip" had always been a try for the Pole. They believed that he'd kept everything a secret so that he wouldn't stampede Peary into hurrying his own expedition and beating him to the punch. Peary hadn't believed them. But now it seemed as if they had been right.

The news angered Matt, just as it upset Peary. How rotten could the man's luck be if, after all the years of striving, he was to be outraced to his goal on this, assuredly his last try? There was only one consolation. Peary had plenty of experience out there on the frozen sea. Cook didn't.

As before, Bartlett took the *Roosevelt* up the four passages and anchored off the northern coast of Ellesmere. And, as before, the men sledged the supplies over to Ellesmere, but this time continued past Hecla to another cape—Columbia. Peary had visited it during his 1906 exploration of the island and had found that it extended a bit farther north into the Arctic Ocean than did Hecla. Here, relieved that they had seen no sign of Cook, the men set up a hut-and-igloo camp. Peary named the camp Crane City, in honor of Zenos Crane, a member of the Peary Arctic Club who had contributed $10,000 to the expedition.

The run north was scheduled to begin on March 1, 1909. On the day before, Peary and Bob Bartlett hiked to a summit behind Crane City for a last check of the frozen sea. When they returned, Peary said that the ice looked as rough as ever. But then he smiled and added that the northern sky was free of what he called "vapor clouds." Blue-black, they were always to be found above leads in the ice and were caused by the open water steaming in the frigid air. Perhaps the Big Lead would be closed and not waiting to stop him this year.

A few hours later, he sent Bob Bartlett's division north to begin cutting the trail that everyone would soon be following. Then he turned to Matt and instructed him to get a good night's sleep. Tomorrow, Matt's division would be first in line when the expedition started out in pursuit of Bartlett.

Ahead lay the last chance to reach the North Pole.

3.

Matt awoke at 5:30 in the morning. He lay for a moment in his sleeping bag while his eyes cleared and the excitement of this March 1 gripped him. Then he was on his feet and reaching for his furs.

Less than an hour later, warmed by a hot breakfast, he walked outside. A hard wind from the east blasted him. The temperature was down to 50° below zero. But the weather was clear. He grinned, knowing it would be a good day for travel.

The sledges had all been placed in a line yesterday. There were nods and waves from the hooded men already gathering at the upstanders. He couldn't help but feel a surge of pride when he saw his own division of five sledges standing at the head of the line.

His four Eskimo drivers were waiting for him. With Kudlooktoo, he gave the loads and the dog teams a final check. Then the two of them walked out a short distance in front of the rigs. There, etched deeply in the ice, were sledge tracks and, in rough spots, the hackings of pickaxes. The trail cut by Bartlett's pioneer party would be easy to pick up. Very soon now, including Bartlett's group, Peary would have five white men, one black, seventeen Eskimos, eighteen sledges, and 133 dogs out on the Arctic Ocean.

Eskimo and black man stood together for a moment. Suddenly, Matt was remembering a tiny child of years ago—the little boy who had slept at the foot of his bunk in Anniversary Lodge. Never in his wildest imaginings back then had he ever thought that one day the two of them would be heading toward the North Pole . . .

They went back to their sledges. Peary came through the gloom, walking with that peculiar shuffle of his. The shrieking wind made all talk impossible. Peary merely gave the rigs a quick but expert glance, clasped Matt's outstretched hand, and signaled him ahead. Whips cracked inches above the teams. The division moved forward.

Without formality, at 6:30 A.M., the expedition was on its way.

Matt immediately picked up Bartlett's trail. The other divisions strung themselves out behind him, with Peary bringing up the rear so that he could keep an eye out for stragglers. One after the other, the sledges crossed the ice spreading out from Cape Columbia. Within a quarter mile, they reached the point where the ice of the Arctic Ocean, driven by wind and tide, crashed into the solid ice of the land and was battered into the usual nightmare of hummocks and pressure ridges.

Gritting his teeth, Matt worked his way through the tumbled ice. Even though the pioneer party had done a good job, he and his Eskimos had to break out pickaxes and clear a wider path for themselves. The wind was fiercer than ever out here at the edge of the sea and it whipped their breath away as they chopped at the ice. The work left them limp and gasping.

Soon, the rough ice began to take its toll of the sledges. Matt's was the first to break, its frame splitting all along one side as it came thumping down the slanting wall of the fifteen-foot-high hummock. He pulled over, saw what had to be done, and began the repair job by boring a series of holes in the frame. Long minutes later, he finished things off when he threaded a sealskin thong through the holes and then pulled it tight to lash the frame back together.

After all the years of sledge repair, he thought it a simple job. Only one thing bothered him: he couldn't get the sealskin thong through the holes without first removing his gloves. With the temperature at 50° below zero, he could only work for a few seconds before his fingers began to freeze. He'd then have to shove his bare hands up through his sleeves and hold them locked in his armpits until some tingling life returned. All the divisions bumped past as he crouched on the ice.

When he was finished, he ran his sledge up to the head of the line, only to encounter more trouble. Another of his division's rigs was damaged. He pulled over to help with the repairs, freezing his fingers yet again. Then bad luck hit for the third time. Somehow, Kudlooktoo's sledge slipped away and bounced over a jagged outcrop of ice. It ended up split right down the middle and with one of its upstanders completely torn away. Matt had to send Kudlooktoo back to base camp for a new rig.

By the end of the day's march several hours later, Matt was telling himself that he'd had enough of broken sledges to last him for the rest of the trip. After hearing Peary announce that they'd made about ten miles,

he built a small igloo and crawled into it for the night. His whole body
ached for some sleep.

But sleep was a luxury that no one enjoyed that night. With the wind
screaming, the temperature dropped to under 50° below zero. The men
could doze for only a few minutes at a time. Then they had to get up and
move about, swinging their arms and pounding themselves to keep from
freezing to death.

The next day started poorly, with Matt's division axing its way through
still more hummocked ice. Word came to him, though, that his bad luck
with the sledges had transferred itself back down the line to Donald
MacMillan. MacMillan's sledge and its 1,000-pound load had plunged
into a deep hole in the ice. He and his Eskimos had really sweated pulling
it out. All the while, his dogs had infuriated him. While he slaved away,
they had frolicked on the ice, actually seeming to enjoy his predicament.

Matt grinned; if he knew Eskimo dogs, they had indeed been happy
about the whole thing. But the grin faded as he looked ahead. After clear
skies since Peary had looked north from above Crane City, a dark cloud
—unmistakably a vapor cloud—was boiling in the distance. There was
open water somewhere ahead, steaming in the frigid air.

Was it the Big Lead, threatening again to stall Peary? No, it couldn't
be. They were still too far below 84° North.

While watching the cloud, Matt broke out of the hummocked ice. He
found himself in an area of old floes, flat but covered with thick, soft
snow. For the next seven miles, the snow came up to his knees with every
step—even after he had put on snowshoes—and up to the chests of the
dogs. There was no walking here; only a plunging ahead, with the body
bent almost double. All the while, the cloud kept growing larger.

Then Matt saw the lead. He groaned. It stretched across his path for as
far as he could see from left to right. At least a quarter of a mile of
steaming water separated him from the opposite shore. As familiar as he
was with the Big Lead, he knew instantly that this wasn't it. But it might
as well have been. After the terrible experience of 1906, Peary had been

advised to carry small boats, but he had refused, not wanting to sacrifice the rations that their weight would take. The expedition was stuck here until the lead—if ever—decided to close.

He heard the divisions bumping to a halt behind him. Then Peary was at his side and staring across at the far shore. Matt knew the thoughts that must be crowding the man's mind. Had Bartlett's people made it across before the lead opened? Or had the ice split under them? When would the lead close? Only time would provide the answers.

Quietly, Peary ordered the men to make camp. Four igloos quickly took shape. As Matt was helping to finish off the last one, he heard an alarmed shout. He looked up to see MacMillan and Marvin running toward him. MacMillan's furs were drenched and stiffening with icy water.

Matt learned later what had happened: the two men had gone over to the edge of the lead with a line to check the depth of the water, and the thin ice had buckled under MacMillan. He'd plunged into the sea, but had saved himself from going all the way under by grabbing the back of his sledge. Marvin had then pulled him out.

With Peary, Matt hustled the shivering man into one of the igloos. They stripped him down, rubbing him furiously all the while to keep the circulation going, and dressed him in dry clothes. For long minutes, Peary held two icy feet up under his flannel undershirt and against the warmth of his chest. Not once in that time did the explorer flinch.

Again, the expedition put in a fitful night of sleep, with the men awakening and moving about every few minutes to keep from freezing. Then, at five in the morning, an excited Peary had them on their feet. Outside, there was a roar like thunder.

It was a frightening sound, but Matt felt a surge of relief. He recognized it as the thunder of the lead closing. Sometime in the night, the two opposing shores had started to move toward each other. A thin layer of ice had formed in the narrowing channel between them. Now, as they came close together, it was being ground into chunks that were piling

Bob Bartlett (right) stops to rest on the Arctic Ocean ice with his team of trailblazing Eskimos.

atop each other. Soon, they'd freeze into a surface thick enough to walk upon.

The men ate a quick breakfast and then pushed their sledges across the lead. Each rig moved at a dead run, for the ice was yet so thin that it undulated on the swell of the sea and curved eerily underfoot. As in 1906, Peary ordered the men to spread their feet wide apart. Then he kept shouting for them to slide their boots along rather than take actual steps.

Once on the far side, an hour's search was needed to pick up Bartlett's trail. The shifting ice had moved it several hundred yards to the west. Relieved to know that the lead had not swallowed up the trailblazing party, the explorer headed northward.

For the rest of the day and the next, sledging conditions were good and the divisions made fine progress. The temperature was up to 20° below zero. Underfoot was old floe ice, flat and relatively free of snow and obstacles. Matt thought it was the best sea ice he had ever seen.

But he wasn't happy. Up ahead, another great vapor cloud lay across his path. As it came closer, it seemed far bigger than the last. They were still too far south for the Big Lead. Or were they? Perhaps the ocean current had shifted the thing. He wondered . . .

In the midafternoon of March 4, Matt reached an igloo built by the trailblazers. Peary came up and ducked inside to find a note from Bartlett. It informed him that Bartlett's men were camped a mile up the line, stopped dead by open water. The sledges moved on immediately.

The sight that greeted Matt at Bartlett's camp was disheartening. There was the open water, somewhat wider than the last lead, steaming, spreading away endlessly to the right and left. Matt watched Peary shake hands with Bartlett and walk to the water's edge. He heard the explorer say that, really, this obstacle hardly looked any worse than the last; surely, it would close soon. But, to Matt, the voice carried little conviction.

He felt sure that Peary was thinking just what he was thinking—that, regardless of how far south they were, this stretch of water bore an evil resemblance to the Big Lead.

Matt groaned. He had desperately hoped that the Big Lead would stay closed while Peary got to and from the Pole. Though they weren't trapped on its far side this time, it could still kill the man. This was the last run. If the water remained steaming there until the supplies were so exhausted that a farther advance north was out of the question, that would be the end of it all—the end of Peary's dream, the end of his own dream to be there at the Pole with him.

Matt turned back to his sledge. How long? he wondered. How long will we be stuck here?

10. The North Pole
1909

Victory

THE men remained where they were until March 11. For seven long days, they rested themselves and passed the time as best they could. MacMillan and three Eskimos were sent back to Crane City for some additional supplies. Goodsell read from the miniature set of Shakespeare that he had brought along. Bartlett amused himself with his copy of the *Rubiyat of Omar Khayham*. Peary nervously patrolled the edge of the ice, waiting and waiting . . .

The weather, Matt later recalled, did nothing to help Peary's nerves. Had it been foul, perhaps the explorer could have reconciled himself somewhat to the delay. But the air was clear, the wind light, and the temperature between 20° and 8° below zero—all adding up to excellent

Donald MacMillan watched Matt quell a "mutiny" among the frightened Eskimos. He became one of Matt's greatest admirers.

conditions for sledging. Matt estimated that they could be easily making twenty-five miles per day.

The Eskimos became especially difficult to handle as the days dragged on. Frightened as always of the sea ice, they were certain that Tornarsuk had cast an evil spell over Peary. They chattered excitedly among themselves, predicting that the evil would continue even if the lead closed; for then it would only open again and cut them off from the land on the way home. The veterans of the 1906 expedition told their friends terrible stories of how everyone had nearly starved that year. There began to be talk of running away.

Soon after returning with the additional supplies, MacMillan happened to hear such talk by a half-dozen Eskimos clustered on the ice. He hurried to Peary and told him that he thought there was a mutiny in the making. The explorer immediately called for Matt.

Matt handled the trouble simply by stepping into the midst of the Eskimos, listening for a few minutes to their fears of the Big Lead, and then telling them quietly that he would never think of abandoning Peary. Then he looked steadily at each man. No one spoke for a moment. Finally, one Eskimo said that if Matt was staying, so was he.

The admiring MacMillan saw the "mutiny" come quietly to an end.

In the next days, MacMillan gave Matt reason to return the admiration. A perennially cheerful man who loved his Arctic work, MacMillan decided that he must help to take the Eskimos' minds off their fears. He began to organize all sorts of games out on the ice. Before long, he was refereeing Eskimo races, spear-throwing contests, and boxing, wrestling, and thumb-pulling matches. As prizes, he jokingly awarded such treasures as the spars, masts, keel, and rudder back on the *Roosevelt*. The Eskimos knew that they didn't have a chance of collecting them when they got home. But that didn't interfere with the fun.

The lead began to close on March 9. Two days later, Peary was able to wave the sledges across the obstacle. Matt was so relieved to be moving again that the area dead ahead—a region of jagged ice and great hummocks—didn't alarm him in the least. He had the feeling that, with the Big Lead out of the way, nothing could keep the expedition from reaching the Pole.

Peary now had Matt relieve Bartlett of the job of trailblazing for a while. Matt spent the next days opening a path through that jagged ice and over those giant hummocks. At times, the obstacles were so great—some hummocks loomed thirty feet high—that he and his Eskimos had to leave their sledges behind while they pickaxed out a trail. Sometimes, two hours would pass before they returned and moved the sledges forward.

They next found themselves in an area where the ice was webbed with fissures hidden beneath the snow. Time and again, the dogs plunged into

Men and sledges inch their way up and over a pressure ridge. Note the dogs relaxing while the men work.

them, howling when they hit the freezing water. And, time and again, Matt and his Eskimos dashed forward and pulled them out by hand. There was always the danger of a savage bite by one of the frightened animals.

Growing more tired by the moment, the dogs decided that they didn't want to work so hard anymore. They began moving too slowly and taking too much time in starting again after a delay. Matt solved the problem quickly. He cut a king dog out of the traces and whipped him in front of all the teams. This one glimpse of what future laziness would bring was enough for the dogs. They got back to their duties.

Matt later wrote that he didn't like what he'd had to do. It was a brutal tactic, he admitted. But a necessary one.

By March 14, the expedition was up to 84° 29′ North. Peary began to put into effect his plan of sending empty sledges and the most beaten of the men back to Crane City. Because of weakening legs, Dr. Goodsell was the first to be ordered back. Then MacMillan was told that he must go; he had frozen a heel at the Big Lead and now could hardly walk.

Peary thanked both men for all their fine work. He congratulated them for having traveled farther north than any other Arctic explorer except Nansen and the Italian, Umberto Cagni. Each was accompanied back to Crane City by several Eskimos.

Between March 13 and 20, the expedition alternated between rough and smooth ice. In that time, accidents almost claimed the lives of two men. One afternoon, while young George Borup was crossing from one floe to another, his dogs plunged into the water. The sledge started in after them. Borup caught the upstanders and was dragged right to the edge of the ice before he brought the rig to a halt. Then he calmly pulled the animals back to safety, his coolness cheating the Arctic Ocean of a good team and a quarter ton of supplies.

Later, up with Matt's division, Eskimo Ahwatingwah's team crashed through some thin ice. The Eskimo almost went into the water with them. Matt started to rush to his aid, then halted. He knew that the addition of his weight might buckle the ice. He stood in an agony of fear while Ahwatingwah, down on his knees, hauled one dog after the other out of the water.

On March 20, Peary decided to send some more men back. Matt watched closely as the explorer made his selections. He was desperately afraid that Peary might point in his direction. After all the days of trailblazing, he was exhausted. Only last night, he had realized just how weak he and his men had become. It had taken them ninety minutes to build an igloo. Ninety minutes! Not since his first days at Red Cliff had he taken that long to put up a shelter.

But Peary pointed to young George Borup. Then, a few days later, to Ross Marvin. Sent back with Marvin and a sledge were two Eskimos, one of them Matt's Kudlooktoo. Before Marvin departed, Peary warned him to watch out for leads. It was advice that Matt, in the years to come, would remember with a haunting feeling. Marvin turned down trail to tragedy.

2.

The tragedy struck soon after the young man and his companions had gotten back across the Big Lead. One gloomy morning, they entered an area of thin ice that was cut with many small leads. Marvin said that he wanted to scout ahead for a safe path. He nodded and smiled at Kudlooktoo's warning to be careful of the thin ice. Then, leaving the Eskimos and the sledge behind, he disappeared into the mists.

He was out of sight for about an hour. Then the two Eskimos came to a place where the ice was broken into small pieces. They stopped and stared, aghast. In the dark water was a balloon of fur which they recognized as Marvin's caribou-skin coat. The man was dead. From the look of the smashed ice around him, he had crashed through and then had fought savagely before drowning or freezing to death. The air in his boots and clothes kept his body afloat.

Afraid of evil spirits, the Eskimos did not touch him. Their people believed that, when a man died, he immediately resumed his work in the hereafter. And so they ran back to the sledge, fetched Marvin's belongings, and pushed them out on the buckling ice, getting them as close to him as they dared. Then they built an igloo and, still terrified of evil spirits, hid in it all night. By the morning, the ice was healed over. The body was gone.

Years later, a troubling news story came out of Greenland about the death. It reported that Kudlooktoo and his fellow Eskimo had just confessed to murdering Marvin. Kudlooktoo, the story went on, was the actual killer. He had shot Marvin when the American became angry at Kudlooktoo's companion and threatened to abandon him on the ice.

The two Eskimos were never brought to trial because of a legal dispute over who had proper jurisdiction in the case. But Donald MacMillan and other of Peary's men were quick to call the report sheer nonsense. In his book, *How Peary Reached the Pole*, MacMillan explained why.

He said that he and a troubled Matt had heard Kudlooktoo tell the original story of Marvin's death many times. Not once had the Eskimo ever varied the tale, not even when he told it in great detail. Further, Kudlooktoo had always admired and liked Marvin. But he'd never cared for the Eskimo companion. How, MacMillan asked, could anyone ever believe that Kudlooktoo would kill a man he liked to protect someone he disliked?

Despite MacMillan's argument, the rumor that Marvin was murdered by Matt's "adopted son" persists to this day in Arctic lore. Since so many years have now passed, it is likely that no one will ever learn the truth of the matter.

3.

Far to the north of the death site, Peary placed Bartlett in charge of trailblazing again. On March 28, with just about 180 miles left to the

Pole, Bartlett shoved off through rugged ice. Matt and Peary followed in an hour or so. As they traveled, they looked worriedly ahead. Another heavy vapor cloud was staining the sky.

Late in the day, they came upon Bartlett camped alongside a wide lead. They were discouraged by the open water, but didn't have the heart to disturb Bartlett for a talk about it. Exhausted, he was dead asleep in an igloo. He later told Matt that he'd spent the day cutting through some of the worst ice he had ever seen.

With their Eskimos, Matt and Peary built their igloos about 100 yards east of the Bartlett party's. After feeding the dogs and downing some frozen pemmican, they bedded down for the night, only to be awakened in a short time. They were about to live through what was possibly the worst moment of the trip.

Matt came awake with a start. Outside, the ice was crashing like thunder. For an instant, he thought that the lead must be closing. Then he crawled to the entrance of the igloo and looked out. What he saw turned his heart over.

The Arctic Ocean was pitching wildly. It seemed to be trying to push and shove the ice in all directions at once. Over near the lead, the ice was giving way to the terrible pressure and was piling itself up into great hummocks and upturned panels. They were crashing into each other, with some sliding across the tops of others.

Matt gasped. The dogs and sledges were picketed right in the shadow of those rising walls of ice. Yelling for his Eskimos to follow, he headed for the terrified animals. Suddenly, the ice underfoot wrenched and threw him back a step. There was a sound like a cannon shot.

He saw in an instant what had happened. A giant crack had come snaking along the ice. Widening quickly, it scissored a jagged path between the Peary igloos and those of the Bartlett party. In a moment, it cut Bartlett completely off from the rest of the expedition. He was left on a small island of white. It began to drift out into the lead.

Matt could see one of Bartlett's Eskimos across the way, hopping about and waving frantically. Bartlett came crawling out of his igloo. Then Matt had no more time to look. He and his Eskimos were too busy pulling the teams and sledges to safety.

By now, Peary was out of his igloo. The ice underfoot continued to split in all directions. He ran to the edge of the lead. He watched Bartlett's floe drift out into open water. Then, swinging, it turned toward Peary. Instantly, the explorer realized that it would likely brush against his own floe as it swept past. Across the narrowing space, Bartlett was hitching up his teams. Peary yelled for him to come across when the floes touched. Bartlett waved his understanding of the order.

Peary now took a look at his own floe. With splits running everywhere, it was shrinking by the minute. He sighted a larger, stronger floe beyond the igloos and dashed to Matt with instructions to drive the sledges over to it. Matt nodded. The sledges bucked forward. Peary hurried back to Bartlett.

The floes were now so close together that, given a good start, a man could jump from one to another. Bartlett had his Eskimos and sledges drawn up and ready to go. The floes ground together. There was a long scraping sound as Bartlett's island ground its way east along Peary's. Peary and all the men yelled at the same time. The dogs shot forward. One after another, the sledges bucked across the narrow, tearing crack. Bartlett came last, jumping high to bridge the water that was again appearing between the two floes.

Bartlett landed right in front of Peary. As one, they immediately turned and watched the now empty floe drift away toward open water, carrying with it only Bartlett's igloo. Both knew that, had Bartlett been over there, they might never have seen each other again.

Without speaking, they led the sledges to the floe where Matt had parked the rest of the expedition. The men built new igloos and fell into an exhausted sleep. The ice continued to thunder, but the danger was past. The expedition was back together again.

The lead closed late the next day, March 29, and the company moved

On the way to the Pole, a sled is placed aboard a floe and then "ferried" across a narrow lead.

forward. By the close of yet another day, March 30, Matt estimated that they were some 150 miles from the Pole. They had been out on the Arctic Ocean for a month.

Matt found himself holding his breath as the sledges came to a final halt that day. He was certain that one of the most critical moments in his life was at hand. Peary hadn't said a thing, but Matt knew that it was time to send the next—and last—batch of men back down to Crane City. Those who were left remaining would be the ones to go all the way to the Pole.

Every time this moment had come in the past weeks, it seemed to him that his heart had stopped beating. Each time, he'd been certain that Peary would see his exhaustion and point to him. But, each time, he'd seen someone else turn back and his hopes had soared anew. But he had never dared to hope too much. Too much hope could only bring too much disappointment.

He watched Peary walk to Bartlett's sledge. The two men stood talking for a moment. Matt felt suddenly weak. Surely, Peary was telling Bartlett to get ready for the final runs north. He saw Bartlett nod. Now Peary was heading this way.

How, after all their years together, would the explorer break the bad news to him, Matt wondered. Peary had to know how much he, too, wanted to go to the Pole. He steeled himself for what surely must come. He mustn't let his disappointment show . . .

Then he was hearing Peary's words and was having a hard time believing them. Bartlett was to make one more march. Then he'd turn for home. Matt and four Eskimos would be left on the ice with Peary.

4.

Like Matt, Bartlett had been hoping to be chosen for the final party. But now, without complaint, he accepted Peary's decision to send him back, saying that all he really cared about was to have his old friend reach the Pole. Then he set about making his last march a magnificent one. On March 31, he blazed a twenty-mile-long trail over the ice and brought the expedition close to 88° N., about 133 miles from the roof of the world.

Here, just beyond the point that Peary had reached before turning back in 1906, Bartlett shook hands all around. He congratulated Matt on his good fortune and wished him well, and Matt knew that he meant it. Then Bartlett and his Eskimos turned their sledges southward.

April 1 was spent repairing equipment and resting for the first of the next marches. Peary watched his men as they worked and, as he'd done so often in the past days, calculated their strength. Matt looked dog-tired. There were deep lines of wear etched in his dark face. But Peary knew that, as always, he had deep reservoirs of strength left in him. And he knew that Matt's happiness at being a member of the Pole party more than compensated for his tiredness.

Though he had never told him so, Peary had always planned to have Matt on the final party. He had mentioned this to MacMillan back at Crane City, saying that he couldn't leave Matt behind, not after twenty years of loyal work, and adding simply, "I can't get along without him." But, even though it meant keeping Matt in a terrible suspense, he'd said nothing to the black man. Had he spoken and had Matt then given out on the trail and been sent back, the disappointment would have been too great.

As for the four Eskimos, they were the cream of the crop, the most tireless ones and the ones least afraid of being so far out on the ice. Three—Seegloo, Ootah, and Egingwah—were Peary veterans. The novice was Ooqueah, a bright-faced young man. But he was a hard worker and eager to please.

The others said that Ooqueah's ambition was grounded in love. Back home, there was a young lady whose hand he hoped to win in marriage with all the rewards he earned from Peary. Matt felt that he was simply a hard worker by nature. The young lady was Annadore, the daughter of Ikwa, the first Eskimo to come to work for Peary so long ago at Red Cliff House.

In all, Peary was satisfied with his people. And he was satisfied with his own condition. So that he'd be fit for the final marches, he'd conserved his strength throughout the trip. He'd ridden his sledge whenever possible. He'd avoided the arduous work of pickaxing the ice. And to spare his eyes, he'd had his men make the daily solar observations that ascertained the latitudes reached.

If ever he had been ready for the Pole, he was ready for it now.

He shoved off on April 2, taking the lead for the first time. Ahead were five marches, each planned to average twenty-five miles. Peary calculated that the fifth would end at noontime, enabling him immediately to take a solar observation to determine if he was exactly at the Pole. If anything went wrong—if any delay was encountered—he figured to double the final march. But delays really didn't worry him. On the sledges was enough food for sixty days.

Peary's spirits were high that April 2. Good fortune seemed to be with him. Sledging conditions were excellent, with the ice underfoot old and

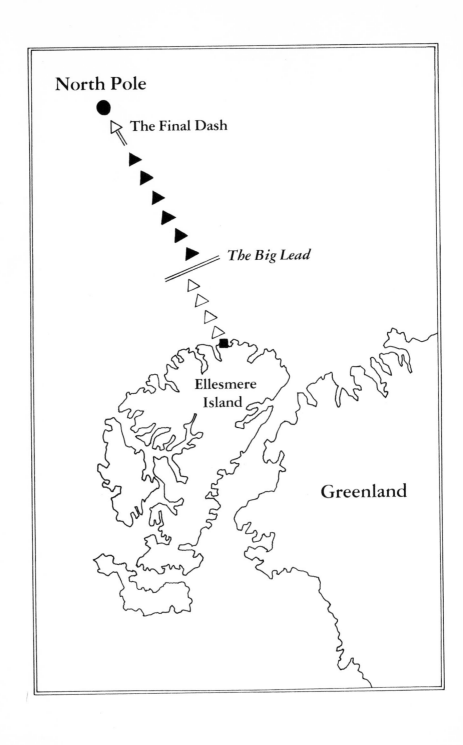

North Pole

The Final Dash

The Big Lead

Ellesmere
Island

Greenland

hard, level, and free of hummocks and ridges for long stretches. There was a brilliant sun. The wind was blowing steadily but not hard. The temperature stood at a comfortable 25° below zero.

Following with the sledges and Eskimos, Matt thought that he had never seen Peary in finer form. Now that the great goal of all the years was within reach, the explorer seemed young again. He walked with giant strides, the miles slipping away beneath him. Matt later wrote that, whenever camp had to be made in the next days, Peary halted reluctantly and gave his people just time enough to get soundly asleep before rousing them up. Matt was sure that Peary didn't sleep an hour a day during those final marches. He said that the rest of the group, himself included, became so tired that they started to stumble and fall repeatedly near each day's end.

But no one objected to the exhausting pace. Peary himself later remarked that his excitement spread even to the Eskimos. They had come out on the ice for pay and not glory, but now their enthusiasm matched his. They were not certain of why it was so important that he reach the Pole. It was enough for them to know that it was the dream of his life and that victory was close at hand.

The march of April 2 lasted ten hours. At its end, Peary turned to Matt, who had a knack for gauging distance, and asked him how far he thought they'd come. Matt estimated twenty-five miles. That was good enough for Peary. Still saving his eyes, he took no solar observations during most of the five marches, depending instead on Matt's intuition.

On April 3, both Peary and Matt ran into the sort of trouble that might well have proved fatal. With the explorer still in the lead and setting the pace, they came to a lane of open water cluttered with floes. Peary crossed over, and a half hour later Matt arrived with the sledges. Slowly, cautiously, he and the Eskimos worked the rigs from floe to floe. Suddenly the block of ice on which he was standing slid out from under him and he plunged into the freezing water. Instantly, he was splashing mightily, grabbing first for the ice and then for the upstander of the sledge, failing both times because his heavy mittens wouldn't give him a secure grip. Before he had a chance to shout for help, Ootah came bounding across the ice. The Eskimo caught him by the nape of the neck and hauled him to safety.

Henson changed boots immediately and beat the water out of his airtight bearskin trousers, but he did not tell Ootah that the Eskimo had saved his life. Ootah didn't expect to be told. Saving each other's life was merely a part of the day's work.

They pushed on and soon caught up with Peary, arriving to find him changing boots. The explorer had turned to watch their approach over ice so thin that it rippled under them. But he himself had broken through and had taken an icy soaking up to the hips.

They rolled on steadily through April 4 and 5. The men were moving in a haze of exhaustion. But they were delighted with their rate of speed. The sky was overcast and a gray shadowless light was spread over the ice. Peary felt the odd, hollow thrill of walking where no man had walked before. He later said that he had never dared to hope for such dazzling progress. Sometimes he would climb up on a hump of ice and stare into the endless whiteness ahead and try to imagine himself already at the Pole.

By the end of the April 5 march, he knew beyond doubt that victory was his. A solar observation showed him to be at 89° 25' N., a scant thirty-five miles from his destination. He bedded down with his men, but he could not sleep. Rest was impossible after all the years of waiting and yearning to reach this desolate spot. He had the party up and marching before midnight. The temperature was 15° below zero. The ice was rock-hard with age. The pace was splendid.

Matt blazed the trail next morning, April 6. He realized that they had reached journey's end when the company halted at 10 A.M. He saw Peary, after directing the Eskimos to build some igloos, open his fur coat and remove a small package from within. Peary opened the package, slowly, carefully, and Matt recognized its contents immediately. It was the taffeta flag that Jo had made eleven years ago, in 1898. This, then, was to be the final camp, the "farthest north" camp. They were at the roof of the world.

Earlier in the journey, Peary had assigned numbers to his camps. Of late, he'd been naming them in honor of certain Arctic greats. There had been, for instance, a Camp Cagni and a Camp Nansen. Knowing this was to be the most important camp of all, Matt hurried to Peary and asked what it was to be called. Camp Peary perhaps?

Peary shook his head. His voice was full of excitement. This was to be Camp Morris K. Jesup, "the last and most northerly camp on the earth." The honor had gone to a great friend, the founder of the Peary Arctic Club.

Matt watched Peary fasten Jo's American flag to a staff and thrust it into the roof of his igloo. At first, it hung limp in the gray, dead air. Then a breeze, rising steadily out of nowhere, caught it and spread its brilliant colors against the lifeless sky. Matt always remembered how a wave of great pride had washed through him at the sight of the flag flying at the top of the world. He gathered the Eskimos together and, on cue from Peary, led them in three cheers. The sledge dogs cocked their heads in surprise.

In any setting, the flag was a remarkable thing to see. Tattered and worn, with squares cut from it for all of Peary's "farthest north" camps, it gave mute evidence of one man's long and unceasing struggle to reach a single goal.

Peary now instructed Matt and the Eskimos to build him a shelter behind which, protected from the flying drift of the snow, he could take a solar observation. They put up a semicircle of ice blocks, with an opening facing the sun. At noon, Peary stretched out on his stomach, his sextant in hand, and a piece of tissue paper for making his calculations set down near his face. Matt placed in front of him a pan of mercury to be used as an artificial horizon. Several minutes later, Peary raised his head. Their camp was at 89° 57′ 11″ North. They were approximately three miles from the Pole.

Matt removed his right mitten and stepped forward to shake Peary's hand in congratulation. But a strange thing happened. Peary seemed not to see the gesture. Perhaps his eyes were sore from taking the sight. Perhaps some ice drift had blown into them. Or perhaps he was fighting back tears. Whatever the reason, Peary suddenly covered his eyes and turned away, failing to take Matt's outstretched hand.

It is also possible that there was quite another reason for the strange incident, a reason that Matt would not mention until years later.

Further work now remained for the explorer. After a sleep of four hours, he set out to take solar observations from other points. He wanted to be absolutely certain that he actually crossed the Pole. Before leaving, he took time to write a few lines about his feelings at this great moment in his life and in the history of exploration. Into his notebook went the words that he couldn't actually believe that he had succeeded and that a geographical prize of centuries was his. Now that he was here, it all seemed "so simple and commonplace."

His first hike took him ten miles out from camp. A midnight observation showed him to be six miles beyond the Pole.

Returning to camp, he made a series of 6 A.M. observations on April 7. They were done at right angles to the ones previously taken here. The figures placed him about four or five miles from the Pole.

Immediately he left camp, sledging eight miles toward the Pole to be certain of passing close by it. He was back at noon. The observations made at that time showed 89° 58' 37" North. There was but a difference of approximately one mile from the earliest readings. And the mile was in his favor, placing him closer to the Pole.

He packed his sextant away. His observations had left no doubt as to his exact locations. Somewhere on his marches out and back, he had crossed the exact spot that is the roof of the world.

The great work of his life was done.

All that remained now was ceremony.

With his company watching, Peary unfurled an American flag on the summit of a giant mound of ice. Then he posed his people for a photo-

Matt (center) and the four Eskimos in the final party posed for Peary's camera at the North Pole. Matt held the taffeta flag that Jo Peary had sewn for her husband years earlier.

graph. Each man held a flag—Matt the taffeta flag that had flown over Camp Morris K. Jesup; Ootah the flag of the Delta Kappa Epsilon fraternity, of which Peary had been a member since his days at Bowdoin; Seegloo the Red Cross banner; Ooqueah the Navy League flag; and Egingwah the peace flag of the Daughters of the American Revolution.

Next, following the custom of all his "farthest norths," he cut a piece from Jo's taffeta flag. He put it with two notes in a glass jar which he placed in the snow.

The notes read:

90 N. Lat., North Pole
April 6, 1909

Arrived here today, 27 marches from C. Columbia.

I have with me 5 men, Matthew Henson, colored, Ootah, Egingwah, Seegloo, and Ooqueah, Eskimos; 5 sledges and 38 dogs. My ship, the S. S. Roosevelt, is in winter quarters at Cape Sheridan, 90 miles east of Columbia.

The expedition under my command which has succeeded in reaching the Pole is under the auspices of the Peary Arctic Club of New York City, and has been fitted out and sent north by members and friends of the Club for the purpose of securing this geographical prize, if possible, for the honor and prestige of the United States of America.

The officers of the Club are Thomas H. Hubbard of New York, President; Zenas Crane, of Mass., Vice-president; Herbert L. Bridgman, of New York, Secretary and Treasurer.

I start back for Cape Columbia tomorrow.

Robert E. Peary
United States Navy

90 No. Lat., North Pole,
April 6, 1909.

I have today hoisted the national ensign of the United States of America at this place, which my observations indicate to be the North Polar axis of the earth, and have formally taken possession of the entire region, and adjacent, for and in the name of the President of the United States of America.

I leave this record and United States flag in possession.

Robert E. Peary
United States Navy

Finally, he took from his gear a postal card that he had carried up from Crane City. On it he wrote a short message to Jo. It was to be mailed at the earliest moment upon his return to civilization.

Then, just before four o'clock in the afternoon of April 7, he turned to Matt and said, simply, that it was time to go home. He was suddenly very tired. All the yearning that had been in his heart for so many years was now quiet. The dream was no longer a dream. It was a reality.

With only a few words, the sledges turned southward. Matt saw Peary look back. Just once. But, in the eyes as they were again turned briefly northward, he saw the sadness of someone who knows that the great work of his life is done.

Matt knew and understood the sadness. For just now he was recognizing a truth about himself. In helping Peary to reach the Pole at last, in becoming himself the first black man ever to stand at the roof of the world, he had ended the great work of his own life.

11. The Peary-Cook Controversy 1909-1910

The Last Storm

T HE homeward-bound *Roosevelt* stopped at the small harbor city of Sydney, Nova Scotia, on September 21, 1909. Bob Bartlett joined Matt at the starboard rail as soon as the anchor was down, peered over at the dock alongside, and said that the whole town must have come out to greet the expedition. Matt nodded. It certainly looked that way.

Whether he turned to the right or left, he could see people crowding the dock, some of them pressed so close to its edge that they were in danger of tumbling into the water. Behind them, flags were flying from every building in the business area. Somewhere, a band struck up a lively march. And out in the harbor, the water was jammed with boats of every sort, from dories to yachts, all festooned with banners and pennants. A

Standing in an open carriage, Peary spoke to the crowd that welcomed him at Sydney, Nova Scotia, on the way home from the Polar triumph.

great roar of welcome exploded on all sides as Peary stepped on deck and led his people down the gangway to be greeted by Sydney's Mayor.

Following close behind the explorer, Matt couldn't help but think: it's really different this time. In the years of failure, Peary had always returned to quiet, sympathetic welcomes. There had been newspaper reports of his adventures—in fact, they'd made his name a household word everywhere—but never any great public furor, no matter how close to the Pole he had gotten. But, just a few days ago, he'd stopped at Labrador. He and his men had telegraphed the outside world of their triumph. Messages had gone to loved ones, the Associated Press, *The New York Times*, and the Peary Arctic Club.

And now here was this roaring, happy crowd. Indeed, it was all very different.

Then, with a sudden smile, Matt told himself that the tumult wasn't the only thing that was going to be different about this return. Never before in all his years with Peary had he come back to a home of his own. He'd always stayed with friends or rented a room until he found a job. But this time, down in New York, there was a home waiting for him, an apartment in the Harlem section of the city. And waiting there was Lucy.

Lucy.

His face softened and he forgot the people who came surging around him with congratulations. Then he only half-heard the Mayor's speech of welcome, half-saw the triumphant march through town, and half-tasted the formal dinner that followed. In his mind, there was only room for his wife.

He had been stationed aboard the *Roosevelt* at the time of their wedding on that September day in 1907. He'd been building sledges and serving as caretaker while the ship was being provisioned and refitted for the 1909 voyage. Now he remembered how he had wondered if Lucy would object to having her new husband go traipsing off to the Arctic for a year. But she turned out to be a woman just like Jo Peary. Matt, she

Seated on one of the sledges that made its way across the Arctic Ocean ice are (from the left) Donald MacMillan, George Borup, Peary, and Matt.

said, had worked long and hard to achieve a great goal with Peary. She wanted him to have this last opportunity to reach it.

They'd had little chance to enjoy any sort of a life together before the *Roosevelt* had sailed. But now, as he sat through the half-tasted dinner, he knew that there would be plenty of time for Lucy and their home—a lifetime of it. The great work was done and all the future years belonged to just the two of them.

Then, suddenly, the thoughts of Lucy evaporated. He began to frown. The great work was done, yes. But there was going to be trouble about it.

Matt glanced along the festive dining table. The people of Sydney were certainly giving Peary a fine welcome. But it was to be expected because he was known and liked here, having often stopped in the harbor on his trips to and from the Arctic. Now the *Roosevelt* was to head for its home port, New York City. Would the welcome there be as friendly?

There was reason to think that it wouldn't be. Because of a strange turn of events in the past days, it might prove to be downright hostile.

Matt saw Peary smiling and talking animatedly to a dinner partner. But, after more than twenty years of work with the man, that smile didn't fool him. Behind it, there was worry and anger. The explorer knew that a storm awaited him in New York City.

It was a storm that had been triggered by that old friend from Red Cliff days—Dr. Frederick A. Cook.

2.

While waiting at Ellesmere to start the 1909 run, Peary and his companions had worried about the Etah rumors that Cook was planning to capture the Pole for himself. But nothing was seen of the doctor anywhere along the coast between the *Roosevelt*'s berth and Crane City, and the men had put him out of mind by the time they sledged north in March. He was completely forgotten when, having made Arctic history, they gathered again on the *Roosevelt* and turned triumphantly for home.

But he came thrusting back into mind as soon as the ship anchored for a stop at Etah. The settlement was full of news about Cook. He'd been there just recently after months of exploration and had sledged south to find a ship that would take him home. And he'd told a friend—Harry Whitney, a wealthy American sportsman who was hunting in the area— that his explorations had taken him clear to the Pole. Peary couldn't believe the story when he heard it from Whitney. There'd been no sign of Cook anywhere on Ellesmere or out on the frozen sea. Whitney must have misunderstood.

But Peary felt a little twinge of worry, especially when he remembered an incident of three years ago. In 1906, after leading an expedition to Alaska, Cook had announced that he'd climbed to the summit of 20,300-foot Mount McKinley while there. It was the highest mountain in North

America and had never been scaled before. However, two companions who had traveled part of the way up with him had felt certain that he hadn't gone clear to the top. Cook had defended himself by promising to produce records proving his feat. But he'd never done so. He'd sailed off on his Arctic expedition instead.

It was possible, Peary told his men, that Cook had become so hungry for glory in recent years that he'd taken to lying about great achievements. But the explorer really couldn't believe this. He'd always found Cook to be an honorable man. Surely, Whitney had misunderstood.

A misunderstanding did seem to be the case when two Eskimos who had been with Cook on his explorations came aboard the *Roosevelt* and told their story. It was a story that, as Peary already knew, began in 1907 when the doctor came north in a steam yacht owned by his financial backer, John Bradley. The yacht left him at Etah with his supplies and sailed home.

With Matt translating, the Eskimos said that the doctor had hired them as drivers when the spring of 1908 dawned. He'd led the way over to Ellesmere Island and then a short distance west to its immediate neighbor, Axel Heiberg Island. After sledging up Heiberg to its northern shore, they all ventured out onto the Arctic Ocean for a hike that ended a few miles later. Cook made camp and stayed there for two days, then marched them south, all the way down to North Devon Island just below Ellesmere and Heiberg.

They spent the winter on North Devon, with their journey ending a few weeks ago when they crossed back over to Greenland.

Matt had the Eskimos repeat their story several times. It remained the same with every telling, with the Eskimos adding the information that they had never been out of sight of land during the entire journey. Matt sighed with relief. The doctor had made a fine trip and had discovered some small islands along the way. But he hadn't come within 400 miles of the Pole at any time. Peary was satisfied that, somehow, Whitney had gotten Cook's story wrong.

That satisfaction was blasted to pieces several weeks later when the

Roosevelt put in an Indian Harbor, Labrador, on September 8 so that the explorer could telegraph the news of his triumph to the world. Stunned, he learned that he was the *second* man in five days to claim the winning of the Pole. After sledging south from Etah, Cook had hitched a ride on a ship bound for Denmark. Stopping en route at the Shetland Islands, he had announced that, on April 21, 1908, he had become the first man ever to stand at the roof of the world.

It was news that hit Peary's men like a savage body blow. Whitney hadn't misunderstood at all. After centuries of lying beyond human reach, the Pole was being claimed by two men within the space of a single week. And, if there was truth in the doctor's claim, it meant that Peary had been beaten to his great goal by more than a year. April 21, 1908!

But it couldn't be true, Matt told himself repeatedly. Cook couldn't have won by more than a year. He couldn't have won at all. Not after what his Eskimo companions had said. And they had no reason to lie. But, after the Mount McKinley incident, there might be reason to question Cook's truthfulness . . .

Then thoughts of Peary's bad luck came pouring in. This was certainly the worst example of it that Matt had ever seen. As part of his payment to the Eskimo workers, Peary had promised to help them stock up on walrus meat for the coming winter when he returned from the Pole. He'd kept his promise, sending his men out to hunt with them for long weeks instead of rushing home with the news of his triumph. And so he'd missed even the pleasure of reaching the newspapers first, with Cook beating him by a hairsbreadth.

When the *Roosevelt* left Indian Harbor and moved on to its next stop—Battle Harbor, Newfoundland—Matt saw that luck grow even worse. The men had tried to console themselves by saying that Peary's telegram would put a damper on the doctor's story. Though Cook had been the first to announce, the world would now wait to see and judge the proof that each explorer presented to back up his claim. In the end,

Peary would surely win out. But, on anchoring at Battle Harbor, they learned that the world wasn't waiting. The news was that, well before Peary's telegram had been sent, the world had taken Cook's story at face value and had made him into a hero.

Just look what had happened! When Cook had finally arrived in Denmark, the city of Copenhagen had started things off by hosting a state dinner for him. Then he'd been received by the King of Denmark, awarded a gold medal by the Royal Danish Geographical Society, and given an honorary degree by the University of Copenhagen. He was presently bound for the United States as a guest of the steamship line. A tumultuous welcome was awaiting him in New York.

Matt now saw Peary lose his temper and take two actions that were to damage the explorer's cause for months to come. First, he fired off telegrams to the United Press and *The New York Times*. He told them both not to take the doctor's claims seriously. He said that, armed with the stories of Cook's Eskimo companions, he would be able to prove that the man had not reached the Pole on April 21, 1908—or on any other date. In the *Times* telegram, he accused Cook of handing the public a "gold brick."

Second, he let his pride and aloofness of old get the better of him when a boatload of U.S. reporters sailed into Battle Harbor to interview him. Fearful of losing control in public at the mention of Cook's name, Peary allowed no questions to be asked. Rather, he presented the newsmen with a terse written statement concerning the Pole run. Reading it tonelessly, he reported that he and his men had departed Crane City with eighteen dog teams; the divisions had provided support during the northward journey, with some breaking trail; he had conserved his strength for the final dash with a selected few men; in comparison with previous attempts, the going had been fast and easy . . .

There was widespread anger across the world in the wake of the telegrams and the statement. Cook was a charming, affable man who, thanks to the press coverage given his Denmark visit, had come to be admired

Jo Peary and her husband aboard the Roosevelt *on the final leg of the journey home to New York. There, a hostile welcome by Dr. Cook's supporters awaited them.*

and liked by people everywhere in just a few days' time. Now they were outraged by the telegrams that bluntly called him a liar. As for the statement—well, it was simply too terse for most tastes.

Whenever Cook had been interviewed, he had given exciting accounts of his adventures, winning all the more public admiration. But Peary's statement contained no mention of adventure, no mention of hardship, no color at all. Many people felt that he had made his trip sound too pat, too easy—actually, as if he were hiding something. As Bob Bartlett even admitted, it looked "fishy." The belief started to grow that Peary hadn't reached the Pole at all.

Matt picked up word of the widespread anger and suspicion during the day of celebration at Sydney. It had been easy to put the news out of mind while there because the people of Sydney were on Peary's side. The same held true when the explorer—accompanied by Jo, Marie, and little Robert, Jr.—was treated to a lavish welcome by his home state of Maine. But, on reaching New York City in late September, everybody aboard the *Roosevelt* was sent reeling.

To begin with, there was the hate mail that came pouring in—hundreds of letters accusing Peary of being anything from a poor sport who couldn't stand the thought of being beaten, to an outright liar in his own Pole claims. Then there were the results of a newspaper poll conducted by the *Pittsburgh Press*. Out of more than 75,000 readers, 73,238 said they believed Cook had reached the Pole ahead of Peary; only 2,814 felt that Peary had won. Just over 58,000 felt that Peary had gotten to the Pole at all.

The anger loomed at its worst on October 2, the 102nd anniversary of the first Hudson River voyage by Robert Fulton's steamboat, *Clermont*. The occasion was marked by a great naval parade on the river, with everything from Coast Guard cutters to passenger steamers and small pleasure craft taking part. Peary, keeping a promise that he'd made before going north for the Pole run, allowed the *Roosevelt* and his men to join the flotilla. As Matt had expected, the day quickly turned into a disaster for the ship.

No sooner did the *Roosevelt* swing into the river than the trouble began. Boos and catcalls echoed across the water from the countless spectators lining either shore. Cook supporters sailed past in small boats, yelling abuses at the men who stood at the rail with Peary. One boat drew closer than the rest and the shouts from its passengers were particularly insulting. Suddenly, young George Borup—the "baby" of the expedition—exploded with anger. He raised a clenched fist and began to shout back . . .

Only to be quickly silenced by Peary. The explorer wanted his men to say nothing; they were to stand in quiet, proud dignity; let the Cook supporters demean themselves with all the shouting. Gritting their teeth and holding their shoulders back, the men did as he wished—all the way up the river to the city of Poughkeepsie and back. Matt always remembered that October day as one of the longest of his life.

As soon as Peary left the *Roosevelt* after the hours of humiliation, he traveled to Maine and secluded himself in the home that he had built long ago on small Eagle Island just off the coast. There, he began writing the story of his Pole run and putting together the records of the solar observations that he had made while crossing the Arctic Ocean. He intended to submit these records to the National Geographic Society as proof that he had attained the Pole. Until the Society studied them and pronounced them valid, he vowed to play no part in the Cook debate. He refused to give newspaper interviews, even to those publications that were on his side. He turned down invitations to testimonial dinners being arranged by his backers and friends. And he ignored a letter from the Broadway showman, William Brady, offering to send him on a lecture tour.

Matt wondered if Peary's silence was a tactical error. By secluding himself away, the explorer left the way open for Cook to gain more friends and admirers. And the doctor did just that—by going on a lecture tour, by happily attending testimonial dinners, and by writing the story of his Arctic journey. The New York *Herald* newspaper paid him $24,000 for the right to publish it. By contrast, Peary struck thousands of people as being a sullen, secretive man.

As soon as Peary retired to Eagle Island, the members of the expedition were free to go their separate ways. Dr. Goodsell resumed his medical practice. Borup and MacMillan headed for their homes, the latter with thoughts about going north one day to explore the Arctic again. Bob Bartlett returned to sea. And Matt?

He found himself without a job. It was, of course, a predicament that he was accustomed to by now. With the exception of the time he'd spent aboard the *Roosevelt* as caretaker and sledge builder before the 1906 run, there had never been the money to keep him on the Peary payroll

Matt soon after coming home from the North Pole.

between expeditions. But it was a predicament new to his wife. It angered and shocked her.

Lucy was angry because she felt that Peary, once her husband's services were no longer needed, had cast him aside without a second thought and without even using his great influence to help Matt find a job. Hers was a criticism that was to be echoed in future years by critics of the explorer, even after it was learned that he once wrote several job recommendations for Matt. If Matt himself felt that he had been discarded—especially after having sacrificed a good job at the American Museum of Natural History to help Peary—he never said so, at least not in public.

And perhaps he never thought so, for his own ambition to bring honor to his people through his work with Peary had been a chief factor in his decision to leave the Museum.

As for her shock, Lucy had always assumed that somehow her husband would make a great deal of money out of his part in the Pole venture. Now she was shaken to learn that the Peary Arctic Club was able to vote a bonus of just $250 for each member of the expedition. Beyond that small amount, Matt had no more than a few dollars in the bank. His salary in all the years with Peary had never risen above $25 a month.

And so Matt went job hunting. At age forty-three, after having stood at the crown of the world, he took a job moving cars and working as a handyman in a Brooklyn garage. His salary was $16 a week.

Then showman William Brady, annoyed that Peary hadn't even answered his letter proposing a lecture tour, entered Matt's life. The cigar-smoking promoter said that there was great public interest in what the black man had done in the Arctic, and he wanted to send Matt touring the country in Peary's place. At first, having no experience as a speaker, Matt didn't like the idea at all. But Lucy insisted that he would do a good job. She reminded him of how he had entertained everyone with his Arctic stories on the night they had first met at George Gardner's home.

Because of her faith in him and his desire of old to bring honor to his people—not to mention the very pressing need for money—Matt finally agreed to Brady's proposal.

Peary erupted like a volcano when he learned of the coming tour. For years now, he had required that all his men—Matt included—agree not to speak publicly or write about an expedition until he himself had done so; as leader, he felt that he had the right to be heard first and to have a clear shot at the profits his talks and books could earn. Further, the explorer wanted his men to remain silent with him until his claim to the Pole was established. Their talk could only inflame the Cook controversy and perhaps worsen matters.

There may have been yet another reason for Peary's fury, one that went back to that strange moment at the Pole when the explorer had turned away from Matt's extended hand.

In the latter part of his life, Matt told a friend—Dr. Herbert M. Frisby—a story of the arrival at the Pole. It was one that he had kept to himself for years. Matt said that, on that memorable April 6, Peary had directed him to travel on ahead and break trail. When he reached a certain point, he was to stop and wait for the explorer. But, in his excitement, Matt had sledged on beyond the point and had been waiting at the farthest north campsite when Peary came up.

Peary, thinking that Matt had betrayed him and beaten him to the Pole, was furious. He took the solar observations and then deliberately turned his back on Matt's outstretched hand. Matt said that Peary never forgave him for what had happened. From that time on—throughout the entire journey home—Peary never talked to him except when it was absolutely necessary to do so.

If indeed Peary had felt betrayed that April day and cheated of his great goal—even after the observations showed him yet to be a few miles from the Pole—then the coming lecture tour must have looked like a double betrayal.

The outcome was that Peary flatly ordered Brady not to send Matt on the tour.

Now it was Matt's turn to be angry. Perhaps the order struck him as being too high-handed. Or perhaps the need for money was too great. Or perhaps Matt felt that he had played such a vital role in the expedition that he was entitled to speak out. Whatever the reason, he joined Brady in ignoring Peary. The situation then ended on the most dismal note possible for him.

The furious Peary stopped in New York during a business trip. He summoned Matt to his hotel room. There, his voice cold and formal, he said that their association was at an end.

The words stunned Matt. He had expected anger, yes. But not the total breaking of a relationship. After all, he hadn't actually reached the Pole ahead of Peary, but only the farthest north campsite. And, after all, he had never told—and wouldn't tell for years—the story of that April day. And, above all else, there were all the years of common effort. Didn't they mean something? In this time of crisis for Peary, apparently not.

Briefly, Matt wondered if Peary, down deep inside, had ever thought of him as anything but a servant. Then he nodded proudly and turned away, knowing that the greatest chapters in his life had closed in one bleak moment.

Though saddened by the break, Matt nevertheless departed on the lecture tour. The next months saw him, dressed in a tweed suit of stylish cut, address audiences all across the country. Starting with talks in Connecticut and New York, he traveled to such Midwestern cities as Chicago and Columbus, Ohio, and then went on to California for stops at Los Angeles and San Francisco.

Back in Maine, Peary began to establish his claim to the discovery of the North Pole. In late 1909, he sent a complete record of his solar observations to a special subcommittee of the National Geographic Society. The committee members, three in all, were experts in the determination of latitudinal and longitudinal positions. A thorough study convinced them that the explorer's records were complete and accurate. There could be no doubt, they reported, that he had reached the North Pole.

The Society responded to their report by immediately striking a special medal for Peary in recognition of his great achievement. To Bob Bartlett for his part in the expedition went the Society's Hubbard gold medal.

Next, the Peary records were sent to the Royal Geographical Society in London and to the U.S. Coast and Geodetic Survey. At the end of independent studies, both groups said the same thing: they agreed with the findings of the National Geographic Society.

By early 1910, there was little doubt left among scientists that Peary had reached the Pole. Words of congratulation and praise began to pour in from universities and scientific societies across the world.

But the questions still remained about Cook. Peary had attained the Pole, yes. But had Cook beaten him there? Or had Cook gotten there at all?

Cook now began to help Peary's cause by behaving suspiciously. A number of scientific organizations asked to see *his* records, but he seemed very reluctant to produce them. For too long a while he kept saying that he needed more time to prepare them. And then, when at last he did send them to the University of Copenhagen for study, they turned out to be a 61-page report of his journey, a report that was very much like the story he had written for the New York *Herald*. Unlike Peary's records, the report contained no firm data on Cook's solar observations.

The University that had so quickly awarded him an honorary degree just a few months ago now had to suffer the embarrassment of announcing that the doctor's report contained no real proof that he had reached the Pole. The University officials weren't just embarrassed; they were angry as well. For, while studying the report, they had asked to meet with Cook so that he could personally answer some of their questions—only to learn that he'd disappeared. Rumor had it that he was hiding in shame or, worn out by the controversy, was traveling somewhere under an assumed name.

Then came more disturbing news. First, the newspapers reported the confessions of two men in Brooklyn; they said that Cook had paid them to supply him with faked solar observations for his report. Finally, topping everything off, there was the action taken by the Explorers Club in New York City. Both Peary and Cook were members. In fact, Peary had served as president a few years earlier.

Ever since 1907, the Club had been trying—in vain—to get Cook to present evidence substantiating his claim of having reached the summit of Mount McKinley. Now, to settle the matter, the Club took testimony from the two fellow climbers who had long doubted his word. They said that they had recently followed the doctor's route up the mountain and had found that it ended far below the summit. The testimony resulted in the Club dropping Cook from its membership rolls.

Cook's disgrace was now complete. He stood exposed as a fraud. Peary's expedition was acknowledged as being the first and only one to reach the North Pole. His place in Arctic history was at last secure.

Yet even after all these developments, Cook was still held in esteem by great segments of the public, thanks in the main to his personal charm. Thousands of people continued to believe in his claim to the Pole for years, even after he was arrested in 1923 and sent to prison on charges of mail fraud in connection with an oil promotion in Texas. On his release, he faded from public view. He died in 1940.

Once Peary's claim to the Pole was established, many honors came his way. The Royal Geographical Society in London awarded him a special gold medal. New York City hosted a demonstration in his honor at the Metropolitan Opera House; a highlight of the evening was a congratulatory message from President William Howard Taft. Then, in March of 1911, Congress recognized his triumph by passing a bill that retired him from the Navy with the rank of Rear Admiral and with an annual pension of $6,500. The bill, however, did not pass without the loud and embarrassing objections of many Senators and Representatives who still believed in Cook.

But what of Matt? He had struggled all those years in the Arctic to bring honor to his people. Now that the great work was done, had he succeeded?

12.

The Closing Years

AT the time of Peary's retirement, Matt was just completing his lecture travels. He returned home thin and drawn, saying that the tour had been far more taxing than the one made back in 1893 with Peary and the six yelping dogs. In fact, for the rest of his days, he would claim that it had been one of the most nerve-wracking experiences in his life. That was quite a statement from someone who had faced the dangers of the Arctic Ocean.

But, from the very beginning, Matt knew that he'd just as soon put up with the Big Lead as with a theater full of strangers all staring up at him. At first, he was so nervous and so inexperienced in the art of speaking that he couldn't muster enough of a voice to be heard by everyone.

Brady, chewing a cigar the whole time, worked with him before each of his first performances and helped him to build his confidence.

The efforts soon began to pay off. By the end of the tour, many of his listeners were saying that he was an interesting and entertaining speaker. Down deep inside, he never really quite believed them.

Nervousness and inexperience weren't his only problems. Brady had been certain that there would be a great public rush to see the black man who had traveled with the controversial Peary. As things turned out, this wasn't the case at all. Though some performances were well attended, most attracted disappointingly small audiences. Either a dislike of Peary kept the people away or they just weren't interested in what a black man had to say.

The situation added to Matt's discomfort. He had worked those long years in the Arctic to help bring honor to his people. Now how could there be honor for them if practically no one was willing to listen to what he had done?

And there was something else—the hostility that came from Dr. Cook's supporters. More often than Matt liked to remember, there were Cook believers out in the audience. Matt could hear them jeering whenever he spoke highly of Peary—as he invariably did—and described the man's abilities as an explorer and a leader. They always came armed with questions meant to trap him into saying something that would humiliate or discredit the explorer. Often, they asked questions aimed at showing that Matt knew little about solar observations (which was the truth of the matter) and so could never have known for himself whether Peary had actually gone all the way to the Pole.

The barb that hurt most of all was the widespread accusation that Peary, rather than taking Bartlett on the final run, had chosen Matt because he was an "ignorant Negro" who would blindly accept "Massah Peary's" word that they had reached the historic goal.

He felt a wave of gratitude and pride, however, when every man in the expedition sprang to his defense. Peary himself, forgetting his anger, joined in to say that Matt had been selected because he was the best dog driver of the lot. Bartlett said that he would have been thrilled to make the final run but that he realized Matt was a better dog driver than he. He added that he thought Peary had used good judgment in choosing Matt.

Young George Borup praised Matt as a jack-of-all-trades in Arctic work and a master of them all. He argued that Matt, because of his years of northern training, deserved to be chosen for the run.

Donald MacMillan, who would one day become Matt's greatest champion, said much the same thing. Then, years later, in his book *How Peary Reached the Pole*, he went even further. He traced Matt's long history with Peary, from the 1891-92 Greenland expedition to the 1909 run. He went on to say that, of all the *Roosevelt*'s men, Matt was the one closest to the hearts of the Eskimos, the one who spoke their language, and the one who had built all the sledges used on the Pole run. Mac-Millan concluded by saying that Peary owed it to his backers to take his very best and most experienced man on the final dash. The explorer had done exactly that.

Exhausted but heartened by the praise of his colleagues, Matt came home from the tour in early 1911, having earned $2,800 for his efforts. For him, it was a sizable sum, but it was just a fraction of the amount that Peary's 1893 talks had brought in.

Matt rested for a time and regained his strength. Then he began to talk with Lucy about his disappointment at having earned so little money and, in particular, at having won no recognition from the white public. He wondered what he could do now to solve these problems. Together, the man and wife found an answer. With Lucy's help, he got down to a new adventure—the writing of a book about his Polar experiences.

Just before completing the manuscript, Matt set his pride to one side and mailed a letter to Peary. In it, assuring the explorer that he was writing about him in a complimentary manner, he asked if Peary would prepare an introduction to the book. Peary, once again dismissing his own anger, agreed to do so, though his letter of reply was unmistakably brusque in tone. Then, after seeing the manuscript, he took yet another step. He recommended it to the Frederick A. Stokes publishing firm.

The book, titled *A Negro Explorer at the North Pole*, came out in 1912. In the introduction, Peary wrote that race, color, and background mean nothing when a man has determination and intelligence. He went on to say that Matt's long work in the Arctic and his contribution to winning one of the world's great prizes for his country was a credit to and a "feather in the cap" of his race. While agreeing with what he said, some people today find the introduction coolly worded and, at times, condescending in tone.

Unfortunately, the book did not sell a great many copies. Perhaps interest in the conquest of the Pole and the Peary-Cook controversy was waning by the time it came out. Perhaps people were turning to other matters. Or perhaps, as had seemed to be the case on the lecture tour, they just weren't interested in what a black man had to say. Whatever the case, again Matt had failed to win the honor he sought for his people.

Though a disappointing seller, the book did have a long life. It is still to be found on today's library shelves, under its revised and modern title, *A Black Explorer at the North Pole*.

Peary's graciousness in helping to have the book published did much to heal the rift between the two men. But they did not see each other in the next years. Then, in early 1920, when Peary was sixty-two years old and desperately ill with pernicious anemia, he called for Matt. Matt hurried to him for a quiet reunion and a talk of their times together.

A few days later, on February 20, the explorer was dead of a disease that, to this day, remains without a cure. Matt had just finished helping Lucy with the evening dishes when he picked up the newspaper and learned of the death. He walked swiftly to the bathroom, locked the door, and turned on all the water taps. But, even then, Lucy could hear his sobs.

Matt's eyes were dry and his face calm again when he came out of the bathroom. After all their work, their failures, and their triumphs, the rift with Peary had been difficult to bear. It was good to know that, in the closing days of the explorer's life, the bad times had been forgotten.

Matt sat down and did his last job for Peary. He wrote a letter of condolence to the explorer's family.

2.

Though the book and the lecture tour won little attention from the white world, Matt's own people paid him great homage for his part in the conquest of the Pole. In 1909, the Colored Commercial Association of Chicago presented him with a gold medal. The Boston Chamber of Commerce followed with a silver loving cup. A safety razor in a gold-stamped leather case from an admirer. Near year's end, the black community in New York City organized a testimonial dinner in his honor; in the course of the evening, he was presented with a gold watch from Tiffany's.

The awards and the recognition of his people were deeply appreciated. But, following the writing of his book, Matt was faced again with the need for a job. Charles Anderson, a prominent black politician who had spearheaded the preparations for the testimonial dinner, came to his aid. Anderson held the position of Collector of the Port of New York, and he wrote a letter to President Taft, urging that Matt be given a government post in gratitude for his services to the country.

Taft granted the request. But the job that came Matt's way was not one that Anderson felt was up to his capabilities. Nevertheless, Matt took it. At age forty-six, gray now at the temples, he became a messenger boy at the U.S. Customs House in New York City. He earned $900 a year at the start, but in time the salary was raised to $2,000 annually. Matt remained at the Customs House, living in quiet obscurity and adding to his income by working at the Post Office during the Christmas holidays, until his retirement in 1936, at age seventy. At that time, he was awarded an annual pension of $1,020.

Matt's failure to win recognition from the world at large—and especially from the United States government—irked many black and fair-
minded white political leaders. They saw it as a deliberate and inex-
cusable slap, not only at him but at all blacks. Beginning in the late
1920s, they went to work on his behalf, urging the federal government to
grant him the honors that he had so long merited.

Representative Fiorello H. LaGuardia of New York, later to be the
very popular Mayor of New York City, started things off. He called on
Congress to enact a bill retiring Matt immediately from his lowly Customs House job and granting him a substantial pension. A similar bill
was introduced by New York Representative J. C. Gavagan in the early
1930s. Later in the decade, an Illinois Congressman called for a bill
granting Matt a special gold medal.

Working hard to obtain that medal for Matt was his greatest champion,
Donald MacMillan, now a high-ranking Navy officer and well known
for his explorations of the Beaufort Sea west of Ellesmere and its fellow
Northwest Territorial Islands. He argued vehemently that men who had
not accomplished one-tenth of Matt's work had been granted medals or
other honors by the government and private organizations. There was
only one reason why Matt was being ignored. He was black.

MacMillan was absolutely right. All the Congressional bills had been
opposed by whites, especially Southern political leaders, who were reluctant to see black influence grow in any manner. Because of their opposition, the measures were tabled and allowed to die quietly.

Though the government had done nothing on Matt's behalf by the late
1930s, the same could not be said of one highly respected private organization. In 1937, when Matt was seventy-one, the Explorers Club in New
York City granted him a full membership. It was an honor that Matt
treasured, for he loved to drop by the club for chats with the members,
especially his old friend Bob Bartlett. Today, a bust of Matt stands in the
club, a gift of the National Association for the Advancement of Colored
People.

One year later, Matt was named an honorary member of the Academy

In 1944, Congress authorized the issuance of a medal for all the men on the 1909 expedition. Matt received his medal from Admiral Herbert Leary.

of Science and Art in Pittsburgh. Then, thanks much to years of tireless urging by now Rear Admiral Donald MacMillan, the Geographic Society of Chicago struck off a special gold medal for Matt in 1948. It was given to him during a testimonial banquet.

In presenting the medal, the Society cited him as "the first Negro in this country to be honored for scientific achievement in the geographical field." Engraved on the medal were the six unforgettable words that Peary had once spoken to MacMillan: "I can't get along without him."

By the time of the presentation, some recognition had come from the government. But just a small bit. In 1944, on the thirty-fifth anniversary of the Pole run, Congress authorized the issuance of a medal for all the men on the expedition, Matt included. It was small comfort to Matt's supporters and MacMillan—but it was at least something.

Additional recognition came in the next years. He was invited to

In 1954, President Dwight D. Eisenhower heard an eyewitness account of the march to the Pole when Matt visited the White House on the forty-fifth anniversary of the Arctic feat. Lucy Henson proudly stood next to her husband.

Washington, D.C., in 1950 to be honored in ceremonies commemorating the forty-first anniversary of the Pole run. But, now eighty-two years old, he didn't feel up to the journey. The next year brought another invitation, this time to attend ceremonies at the Pentagon. Again, because of the frail health that had come with age, he had to remain at home.

But, in 1954, when he was eighty-seven, he did make his way to Washington to place a wreath on Peary's grave in Arlington Cemetery. Then, accompanied by Lucy, he was driven to the White House for a brief visit with President Dwight D. Eisenhower. With Lucy and the President, he stood in front of a giant globe of the world while photographers snapped their flashbulbs and caught him smiling down—a little wistfully, it seemed—at the roof of the world.

Matt and Lucy lived quietly in New York's Harlem district during the twilight years of his life. Daily, he went for walks and often dropped by the Explorers Club. On Sundays, he attended services at the Abyssinian Baptist Church. He was well known throughout the Harlem area to both adults and children. They often stopped him on the street to ask about his Polar adventures. But, other than answering their questions, Matt no longer talked much about the Arctic. His work there had ended so long ago that surely people weren't all that interested in it anymore. And, besides, he had never been much of a one for bragging.

His health was frail but still good toward the end. When he was in his mid-eighties, he underwent surgery for a hernia and recovered successfully, if slowly. Then, in 1955, he fell suddenly and painfully ill. He was taken to St. Clare's Hospital for prostate surgery. Two days after the operation, he died quietly. He was eighty-eight years old.

It was a chilly March 9, 1955. On that day, forty-five years earlier, Matt Henson and Robert Peary had stood alongside the Big Lead and wondered if it would ever close. When it did, they had marched north to their destiny.

In his lifetime, Matt never received the full share of recognition due him. But, in the years following his death, as was beginning to happen in his closing days, the situation changed. There were many honors for him and thus, as he had hoped, for black people everywhere.

In August, 1956, a U.S. Air Force plane flew over the North Pole. Aboard was Dr. Herbert M. Frisby, the friend to whom Matt told the story of the "handshaking incident" at the North Pole. Now a tireless worker in seeking recognition for the black explorer, he dropped a steel cannister to the ice far below. Contained in it were mementos honoring Matt and Peary, among them the Bible that Matt had carried on the 1909 journey.

Incidentally, in making the flight, Dr. Frisby became the second black man in history to reach the Pole.

Three years later, on the fiftieth anniversary of the Pole's conquest, Matt's home state of Maryland declared April 6 to be "Matthew Henson Day." The city of Baltimore, where he had found a berth aboard the *Katie Hines,* named a new elementary school in his honor in 1963. Many of the artifacts of his Arctic years were placed in Baltimore's Morgan State College and were designated as the Matthew A. Henson Memorial Collection. In New Orleans, the new gymnasium and auditorium at Dillard University bore the name Henson Hall.

Possibly the greatest recognition came in 1961 when Dr. Frisby spearheaded a statewide drive to have the State Legislature pass a bill enabling a bronze tablet honoring Matt to be placed in the State House. It became the first memorial in Maryland to honor a black.

The tablet is headed with the words:

MATTHEW ALEXANDER HENSON
Co-Discoverer of the North Pole
with
Admiral Robert Edwin Peary
April 6, 1909

It then reads in part:

Son of Maryland, exemplification of courage, fortitude and patriotism, whose valiant deeds of noble devotion under the command of Admiral Robert Edwin Peary, in pioneer arctic exploration and discovery, established everlasting prestige and glory for his State and Country . . .

There's no doubt that Matt would have liked those words "established everlasting prestige and glory for his State and Country . . ." But what of that new designation—"Co-discoverer of the North Pole"? As good as he might have felt about being raised from the position of an assistant, wouldn't it have made him smile? For there had always been four other "co-discoverers": his friends and "brothers" of the north, the Eskimos Ootah, Egingwah, Seegloo, and Ooqueah.

He would have smiled and said what he had always known—in fact, what Peary had always known and had mentioned in the introduction to Matt's book: that the capture of the Pole had been the result of three races—Mongolian, black, and white—working harmoniously together toward a common goal. It was a good way of doing things.

A Selected Reading List

If you'd like to read more about Matthew Henson, Robert E. Peary, and Arctic exploration, the following books should prove of special interest:

Andrist, Ralph K., and the editors of *Horizon* magazine. *Heroes of Polar Exploration.* New York: American Heritage Publishing Co., 1962.

Angell, Pauline K. *To the Top of the World: The Story of Henson and Peary.* New York: Rand McNally & Company, 1964.

Borup, George A. *A Tenderfoot with Peary.* New York: Frederick A. Stokes, 1911.

Calder, Ritchie. *Men Against the Frozen North.* London: Allen & Unwin, 1957.

Henson, Matthew A. *A Negro Explorer at the North Pole.* New York: Frederick A. Stokes, 1912; Arno Press, 1969.

Hobbs, William Herbert. *Peary.* New York: Macmillan, Inc., 1936.

Lyttle, Richard B. *Polar Frontiers.* New York: Parents' Magazine Press, 1972.

MacMillan, Donald B. *How Peary Reached the Pole.* Boston: Houghton Mifflin Company, 1934.

Peary, Josephine. *My Arctic Journal.* New York: Contemporary Publishing, 1893.

Peary, Robert E. *Nearest the Pole.* New York: Doubleday & Co., 1907.

———. *The North Pole.* New York: Frederick A. Stokes, 1910.

———. *Northward Over the Great Ice.* 2 vols. London: Methuen & Co Ltd, 1898.

Robinson, Bradley. *Dark Companion.* New York: Robert M. McBride, 1947.

Sykes, Sir Percy. *A History of Exploration.* 2nd ed. rev. New York: Macmillan, Inc., 1936.

Weems, John Edward. *Peary: The Explorer and the Man.* Boston: Houghton Mifflin Company, 1967.

———. *Race for the Pole.* New York: Henry Holt, 1960.

Index

Flags (*cont'd*)
 Jo Peary's, 51, 107–108, 114, 119,
  148, 149, 151
Flashlight, Eskimos' reaction to, 45
Food for Arctic expeditions, 89, 90,
  123
 See also Supply caches
Fort Conger, 109, 110, 112, 113, 114,
  115, 116, 117
Franklin, Sir John, 25
Frederikshaab Glacier, 28
Frisby, Dr. Herbert M., 167, 179, 180
Fulton, Robert, 163
Fund raising, 16, 18, 19, 21, 57, 62–
  65, 107

Gardner, George, 120, 166
Gavagan, J. C., 176
Geographic Society of Chicago, 177
Gibson, Langdon, 22, 23, 30, 41, 51,
  59
Goodsell, J. W., 125, 126, 134, 138,
  164
Greely, Adolphus W., 109, 114
Greenland, 13
 as an island, 19, 56, 115
 expedition to, planned, 17, 18–19
 northeast corner of, 19, 55, 56, 60,
  62, 65, 67, 85, 100, 114
 Peary's first trip to, 16
Greenland coast, description of, 28
Greenland expedition, first, 26–60
 equipment and supplies for, 27
 members of, 34
 newspaper predictions concerning,
  25, 60
 preparations for, 21
 scientists on, 27
Greenland expedition, second, 65–101
 companions chosen for, 65
 disaster on, 74
 Peary's plan for, 65–67, 78, 80
Greenland icecap
 Nansen's crossing of, 18
 Peary's crossing of, 19, 20, 40–41,

54. *See also* Greenland expedition,
 second

Hecla, Cape, 117, 118, 122, 127
Heilprin, Angelo, 27, 32, 33, 53–54,
  56
Heilprin Land, 56
Henson, Lemuel
 death, 5
 family of, 4–5
Henson, Lucy, 156, 157, 173, 174,
  178, 179
 attitude toward Peary, 165
 Matt's lecture tour urged by, 166
 See also Ross, Lucy
Henson, Matthew Alexander, 23, 34,
  68, 151, 157, 165, 177, 178
 "adopted son," 84. *See also* Kudlooktoo
 birth, 4
 book by, 173
 bust in Explorers Club, 176
 cabin boy, 6–7
 carpentry skill acquired, 7, 10, 76
 choice for "final Pole party," 144
 church attendance, 179
 Customs House job, 175
 death, 179
 defense of, by expedition members,
  172–173
 Eskimo name, 39, 69
 explorer, 3, 86, 89, 101
 first job, 5
 "handshake" incident recalled by,
  149–150, 167, 179
 honors for, 115, 175–181
 job experiences, 7–8, 166
 last years, 179
 lecture tour, 166, 168, 171–173
 marriage, 125
 meeting with Lucy Ross, 120
 meeting with Peary, 8–9
 museum employment, 104, 105,
  106, 107
 Peary's anger at, 166–168

About the Author

EDWARD F. DOLAN, JR., a native Californian who now lives just north of San Francisco, was raised in Los Angeles. After serving with the 101st Airborne Division during World War II, he worked as a teacher and then as a newspaperman and magazine editor.

He began writing books in 1958 and his first, *Pasteur and the Invisible Giants*, was published by Dodd, Mead. Since then, he has written more than thirty-five books for young people and adults. His titles include three histories of exploration and fifteen biographies. He has also written numerous magazine articles and short stories.

Mr. Dolan and his wife, Rose, have two children, both grown and married.